GOD's WORK done GOD's WAY

You don't have to make headlines
to make a difference

Subesh Ramjattan, DHL

GREEN WINE™
FAMILY BOOKS

GOD'S WORK DONE GOD'S WAY

You Don't Have to Make Headlines to Make a Difference

Copyright © 2012 by Subesh Ramjattan

Library of Congress Control Number: 2011941506

Ramjattan, Subesh 1951—

ISBN 978-1-935434-60-3

Subject Codes and Description: 1: REL012000: Religion: Christian Life - General 2: REL012040: Religion: Christian Life - Inspirational 3: REL012120: Religion: Christian Life – Social Issues.

Cover Design by Saga Studios Limited, Trinidad and Tobago W. I.

Printed in Australia, Brazil, France, Germany, Italy, Spain, Brazil, UK, & USA and anywhere there is an Espresso Book Machine.

The Press does not have ownership of the contents of a book; this is the author's work and the author owns the copyright. All theories, concepts, constructs, and perspectives are those of the author and not necessarily the Press. They are presented for open and free discussion of the issues involved. All comments and feedback should be directed to the Email: [comments4au- thor@aol.com] and the comments will be forwarded to the author for response.

Published by

GreenWine Family Books

A Division of
GlobalEd Advance PRESS

www.gea-books.com

DEDICATION

To my son and daughter,

Nigel and Michelle,

whose patience and respect for a
"project-oriented" dad remains a source of
encouragement to me.

Perhaps this book,
Doing God's Work God's Way,
will assist their understanding of
my spiritual journey.

Contents

PROLOGUE

A THEOLOGY OF THE DISADVANTAGED

With conversion to Christianity as an adult, Subesh Ramjattan brought with him a varied history. His life narrative included growing up poor with limited opportunities, educational struggles, early illness that included the loss of a kidney, the death of a younger brother, business problems, the use of alcohol, and marriage difficulties. These have all contributed to his theology. This background together with the New Testament picture of a loving and caring Jesus produced a "Subesh" version of a theology of the disadvantaged.

Jesus cared for the little children and demonstrated concern for the poor. He healed the sick, wept at the death of a friend, loved His enemies, took the long view of life, and planned carefully for a legacy of followers to continue His work. This appears to inform the theology of the disadvantaged utilized in the work and ministry of Subesh and his wife, Debra. According to the book The Anapausis Partnership (2011), Debra Ramjattan shared a common background experience, and this informs her support for their work and ministry together.

This theology of the disadvantaged has produced the Bridge of Hope, a safe place for abused, abandoned, and disadvantaged children to grow, develop, and bloom into productive citizens. This theology produced the Anapausis Community to service people of faith in their search for a better life, improved relationships, and ministry. The ministry includes a "quality of life" component shared with couples and individuals struggling with the normal adult difficulties and relationship issues in business and married life. The capstone of this ministry is a four-stage project to serve the needs of the Elderly in Trinidad and Tobago. This is indeed a theology of the disadvantaged with the goal of improving the quality of life for all.

The right theology is a key ingredient of "vision" for a leader in ministry. There must be a balance between affluence and compassion. Wealth or what some call "prosperity" provides the means to be compassionate toward the less fortunate, but without spiritual vision the effort to truly serve others will fail. Doing what is right for the poor and disadvantaged only to avoid leaving them behind, is not sufficient to empower them with hope, opportunity, and promise for the future. A true leader must look beyond the present and see possibilities. This was a reason for the writer of Proverbs to pen, "Where there is no vision, the people perish."(Proverbs 29:18 KJV) That reason seems clear: without a balanced theology and a working philosophy, the ingredient of vision will be missing in leadership and the people will suffer.

There is a classic line by Shakespeare, written for Brutus in Julius Caesar, that speaks to an understanding of this proverb: "There is a tide in the affairs of men, which, taken at the flood, leads on to fortune; omitted, all the voyage of their life is bound in shallows and in miseries..." When vision flows from the soul and overflows the heart into the hands of the leader, the people including the poor are blessed. It appears that Subesh Ramjattan has manifested the key ingredients of spiritual leadership in his ministry to the disadvantaged.

This book is a message to believers of the Christian faith to encourage their participation in the Commission of Christ to develop a life-style of witness and care for the disadvantaged. As believers go about their daily lives they must make disciples and then nurture them in the faith until the converts become both a meaningful home builder and a missionary in the marketplace sharing their witness of saving grace.

—Hollis L. Green, ThD, PhD

This book uses many passages of scripture, most of them from The EVERGREEN Devotional New Testament. Debbie and I are Patrons for the publication of this devotional translation and willingly share this devotional rendering of scripture. The frequent use of scripture was not only to support my words, but scriptures were added because God's Word says things better than this author can provide the language skills to communicate. Be patient and read each passage carefully; the message may not be readily seen. Ask the Holy Spirit for illumination of the Word. God bless you as you read, understand, and share the message of grace and love to all who will listen.

Blessed the nation whose God is the Lord,
Blessed the land where He reigns.
Blessed the people who trust in His Word,
And worship His glorious name.

Elizabeth de Gravelles -- Based on Psalms 144:15

Faith-based Principles Make a Difference

Starting with the Ten Commandments from the Torah and appearing in various forms in other religions to the Golden Rule in the New Testament, we are stewards of both the instructions and the resources God provides. The Golden Rule is so basic it appears in most of the religions of the world. For example:

- **Buddhism** –"Hurt not others in ways that you yourself would find hurtful" (Udana-Vaarga 5,1)

- **Christianity** –"As you would that men should do unto you, do you also to them likewise." (Luke 6:31)

- **Hinduism** – "This is the sum of duty; do naught unto others what you would not have them do unto you." (Mahabharata 5, 1517)

- **Judaism** – "What is hateful to you, do not do to your fellow-man. This is the entire Law; all the rest is commentary." (Talmud, Shabbat 3id)

- **Taoism** – "Regard your neighbor's gain as your gain, and your neighbor's loss as your own loss." (Tai Shang Kan Yin P'ien)

PREFACE

BEHAVING GOD'S WORD

Reading this book motivates me to work with greater diligence in time and commitment of effort. I do not belong to myself, but in service to His Kingdom. He owns the rights to my skills, time, and possessions. We are workers together.

Behaving God's Word is learning. His Word is complete with instructions for successful, stress free living. *God's Work Done God's Way* interprets these instructions for practice.

A flawed technique in sports reduces success and creates frustration with unfulfilled objectives. To correct technical flaws sportsmen surrender to intense practice. Christians are required to yield to intense practice in behaving God's Word.

God's integrity of commitment to His creation commands response. Each man's obligation and positive response to redemption indicates trust in God's integrity. The author refers to Joseph of the Old Testament, identified as a hero of faith in Hebrews 13, who responded to God's integrity when "he spoke of the departing of Israel from Egypt, and gave orders for the removal of his bones," (Hebrews 11:22 DNT).

Positive response to redemption is appropriate initial behavior in signaling our availability to bring comfort to others. Each man is uniquely gifted, prepared for service, and reward- ed in His Kingdom. Failure to volunteer for service leaves gaps. Who will fill your gap? In doing God's work His way, the gaps in the Jerusalem Wall were rebuilt under Nehemiah and all were repaid.

—Paratan Balloo, MBA, DPhil
Vice Chancellor/CEO
OASIS UNIVERSITY

The proceeds from this book will support Olive's House
and the four-stage project for the Elderly.

(See pages 180-185)

Donations Appreciated

INTRODUCTION

I present this book to believers because I see Jesus being perceived as a "spare tire" or "vending machine," and it disturbs me. All the principles and precepts have been laid out in the Holy Scripture. I see two sides to Jesus: one, the redemptive blessings He offers to those who believe; and, two, the obligations of believers toward Jesus. The first one is the easy one. Jesus freely gives, and we willingly accept His blessings. The other side of the coin is the one often neglected. The opportunity to serve and witness is indeed an obligation that most seem to overlook. This book is about those obligations.

I want my brothers and sisters in Christ to live a life with purpose and significance: a life that is large for God. A lifestyle that cares for the disadvantaged and meets the challenge to make disciples is God's plan. God did not save us to be comfortable; He saved us to comfort others. We live in a world with many distractions, and we need to focus on our relationship with Jesus and feed our mind with quality thoughts and values. A better quality of life comes from a better quality of believing and behaving. It is not what we gather, but what we scatter that tells the quality of life we live. And the way we live determines our legacy.

> And be not fashioned according to this age; but be transformed by a new mental attitude, that you may confirm for yourselves what is good, acceptable, and the complete will of God, (Romans 12:2 DNT).

Jesus fulfilled His mandate and finished the work He was sent to do, and the Heavenly Father expects us to do the same. Jesus said, "as my Father has sent Me, even so send I you," (John 20:21 DNT). In the next verse, Jesus told His disciples to receive the Holy Spirit. The Spirit will guide us in doing God's work God's way. Jesus calls us to be a living witness and some of us keep putting it off and saying "tomorrow will be a more convenient day." Satan is happy with this delay, because "later" often becomes "never." We need to step out in faith and answer the call. I believe God qualifies those He calls. It is not ability that God seeks, but our availability. The Holy Spirit will enable each of us to meet our spiritual obligations as long as God's work is done God's way.

In the Hands of Believers

The Godhead has done all they determined to do to redeem the Human race: God gave His Son, Jesus gave His life, and the Spirit is at work in the world convicting humanity of sin, righteousness, and judgment. God leaves the rest to believers. A neglect to share the good news of redemptive grace or a failure to meet the needs of the poor is overt disobedience and is sinful. The ability to serve both God and man remains in the hands of believers. Surely, each believer will have the assistance of the Holy Spirit, the knowledge of Jesus Christ in the Word, and an abiding understanding that God the Father had a plan for the redemption of the lost and that plan includes each believer doing his or her part to share the good news of God's grace. This is the plan to do God's work God's way.

A Workable Plan

Some ask, "What is God's plan?" The behavior of early believers clearly demonstrates a workable plan. God prepares the saint, creates the situation, puts the sinner in the right place, and supplies useable material to present the good news concerning Christ. This is God working with believers to serve individuals at their point of need. This is indeed God's plan: reaching individuals at their point of need at the earliest point of time at the farthest distance from a place of worship. In other words, out where they live and work. Then the process of making disciples begins with worship and steps toward growth in grace and knowledge. This happens not only in places of faith-based worship, but through the life-style of individual believers as they demonstrate a good example in all aspects of their lives. Life-style and personal hands-on sharing of the gospel is truly doing God's work God's way.

Sins of Neglect

To neglect or delay an opportunity to serve the needs of others is to commit the sin of omission. About such oversight or lapse of responsibility, ancient scripture was clear: "Therefore if a man has the **power to do good; and fails to do good it is sinful,"** (James 4:17 DNT). Wrongdoing in any form is literally "missing the mark" and becomes an offense against both God and man. This understanding comes from the early terms used in archery. When the arrow failed to strike close to the center or missed the target altogether, the arrow "missed the mark" and this became known as "sin." There is no excuse for sins of neglect. Such failure may be avoided by doing God's work God's way.

—Subesh Ramjattan

Listen to His Voice

6. Come, let us worship and bow down. Let us kneel before the LORD our maker, 7. for he is our God. We are the people he watches over, the sheep under his care. **Oh, that you would listen to his voice today!** *(Psalms 95:6-7 NLT)*

CHAPTER ONE

FRESH EACH DAY

Experience the Lord Fresh Each Day

To do God's work on earth adequately, each believer must have a regular and organized devotional plan. This requires an understanding of the way God constructed the 24-hour day. If one follows the words of Genesis it is clear that "the evening and morning" described the way God saw the day. This construct is repeated many times in Genesis to establish God's view of the 24-hour day. According to the historical practice of the Old Testament and even the early believers, the day begins the evening before. "The evening and morning of the first day" is a common expression. To experience the Lord fresh each day, one must begin the devotional process before the sun goes down. Believers neglect this concept at their peril. Therefore, the devotions for the day should begin at sundown the evening before and continue at the morning sunrise. For example, Saturday at sundown is the time to prepare for Sunday morning. When one is sleepy and tired entering the First Day of the week and a time of worship, they are not prepared to receive or behave adequately based on the Word. This would be true of each day in the week.

Two Kinds of People

Someone said, "There are two kinds of people in the world." Perhaps this could be said of people in various situations, but when it comes to believers and their spiritual devotions, the two kinds of people could be: (1) those who wakeup in the morning and say, **"Good morning, Lord,"** and (2) those who wake up in the morning and say, **"Good Lord, it's morning."** The second kind certainly would not experience the Lord fresh each day. Hopefully, those who read this book are in the first category and wake up with their heart and spiritual ears open to both the word and worship. Remember, worship is a response to the worth and value of God in your life. How much is God worth in your family, your business, your community, or your church? How do you value God in your daily life? What value does the Bible have for you and your family? The Word will give you tools to fight the good fight against the forces of evil and win.

The Tools to Defeat Satan

The daily reading and behaving of scripture strengthens the family and provides believers with the tools to defeat the forces of Satan that work against the life and witness of all who trust the Word. When you believe the Bible, Satan trembles. When you open it, he stumbles in fear. When he sees you reading the Word of God, he crumbles in despair. When he knows that you are behaving what you read, he folds his tent and flees. And when you share your faith with others, he knows he is defeated, but his cohorts will continue to discourage all those who believe and behave the Bible.

Be God's true subjects; stand firm against the devil, and he will vanish from you. 8. Bow down before God, and he will be near your hand. (James 4:7 DNT)

Spiritual Listening

God placed in each heart a spiritual ear (h**EAR**t); it is with this "ear" that believers listen to God and His Word. As one daily engages in the devotional reading of scripture, the message of the Word is made clear through spiritual listening. This kind of sanctified listening requires one to analyze and act based on the truth they discover in the devotional reading. Believers should not strive or struggle to get the meaning of scripture; they must tune in through spiritual listening to the illumination that the Holy Spirit brings to the reading. A question becomes obvious, where does God's work need me most today? The renewal of the Spirit comes as one listens with the h**ear**t, and the tasks of the day become clear. The believer is now ready and willing to fully participate in God's plan, as the body, mind, and spirit report ready for daily action.

Be Prepared at Sunrise

Prior to the resurrection of Christ, the custom was to "rest from labor," and the view of life was looking back to the difficulties of the past. Now the best practice is to "rest for your labor" and be prepared at sunrise to participate fully in a God-directed life. The evening of rest then prepares one for the duties and hard responsibilities of the daylight hours. Scripture reminds us that "when it was yet dark" on the First Day of the week, Christ rose from the grave to become the Redeemer and Savior of the world. It is appropriate then for believers to prepare themselves before the sun goes down for the opportunities at sunrise and throughout the daylight hours. Could this be why scripture declares, "don't let the sun go down on your wrath?" This is why I recommend evening and morning reading from The EVERGREEN Devotional New Testament. See Appendix A, p. 213

A Positive Attitude

Worry is taking responsibility for something that belongs to others or to God. To waste time and energy looking back at circumstances and being anxious or troubled about something that happened or the anticipation of something bad that might happen is both uncomfortable and unchristian. Believers must have **a positive attitude and be willing to be led by the Spirit on a daily basis.** Otherwise, those who attempt to follow Christ will drift back into their old habits and lifestyle. This makes the Cross and the redeeming power of Christ ineffective in a world that desperately needs both acceptance and redemption. All believers must emphasize the necessity of prayer and thanksgiving to be adequately prepared to influence positive change in the lives of others. A pastor once asked an elderly member how she felt. Her answer, "My condition is pretty good for my condition." The pastor pressed for more information.

Her response, "Well, pastor, I feel better now than I did a while ago."

*Be anxious for nothing; but **under all circumstances by general prayer and specific petition joined with thanksgiving let your needs be known to God**.*   *(Philippians 4:6 DNT)*

Always Positive

Once there was a mother who tried to always be positive. She tried to never say "no." Her young daughter asked, "Mother, may I go outside and play?" "Yes, when your brother gets home from school." Another question from the son, "Mother may I have an ice cream?" "Yes, when we go to the store on Friday." The children grew up, and the daughter visited and made lunch for her mother and asked, "Mother, I made some tea, do you have any ice cubes?" "Yes, but they are not frozen yet" was the positive answer. Would it not be great if we could always be positive? To be positive is to be upbeat, optimistic, constructive, encouraging, sure, clear, confident, and secure. These are the marks of a believer. Such traits provide for a hopeful future that is committed to the Hands of God through a positive faith. The absence of faith brings doubt. There is no place in the life of a believer for doubt.

A Hopeful Future

Believers should not be apprehensive about the future or overly concerned about the past. One gains nothing when negativity overwhelms the possibility of spiritual progress of redemption. God's forgiveness wipes out the sins and short-comings of the past and "blessed assurance" equips believers with a hopeful future. We should all say, **"This is the day the Lord has made. I will rejoice and be glad in it!"** Parents should remember that their children know a lot more than they think. This is a good reason for including the family in spiritual devotions, even some of the lessons adults may have forgotten from childhood songs. This story makes the point!

Children Do Understand

A father was approached by his small son, who said,

"I know what the song "B-I-B-L-E" means!"

His father smiled and replied,

"You know what the Bible means!"

"Yes!" the son replied, "I do know!"

"Okay," said his father.

"What does the Bible mean?"

"That's easy, Daddy..." the boy replied, "It stands for

Basic

Information

Before

Leaving

Earth"

The Truth about the Word

Out of the mouth of a child comes the truth about the
Word. Children do understand much about the Christian way of
life. And they know when parents are shortchanging the family
due to lack of spiritual example and leadership. And experiencing the Lord fresh each day in family devotions is a good way to
keep the lessons garden-fresh on the family table. Most adults
have forgotten that the stories in the Bible are placed there
to teach good lessons. Even the songs children sing have a
message that some adults have forgotten. Do you remember
the words of the children's songs and the lessons they taught?
Perhaps a review of the words to the song "B-I-B-L-E" would
remind parents of the power of the true lesson: **"The Bible is
the book on which all believers should stand."** This is the
way to experience the Lord fresh each day. Here are the words:

The B-I-B-L-E, Yes, that's the book for me;
I stand alone on the Word of God,
The B-I-B-L-E.

Asking God to Bless

Asking God to bless in the biblical sense is to seek a favorable intervention in your life and work. That is, when one seeks God's blessing they seek something beyond their human power to achieve or receive. Since it is God's blessing one should leave the nature of the answer to divine wisdom; this is what Jabez did. When Jabez asked that his coast or territory be enlarged, he probably wanted to enlarge his area of influence, extend his field of mission, increase his area of witness, or even gain a larger gathering of resources. Depending on the Old Testament translation in which one reads the Prayer of Jabez, they find different words for his petition. What is clear is that Jabez wanted to change the concept of "No gain without pain." He wanted gain not pain. He wanted to change his self-image. Jabez was named because of his mother's birth pains, and now the past experiences of others were impacting his current self-image. Jabez requested divine intervention to change his life for the better by opening the way to a blessed future. Why not ask God to bless your future? The answer is just a prayer away!

Be with Me in All I Do

Jabez did not want to dwell on the past, but prayed with hope and anticipation for a better future. He wanted to live a more effective and expanded life. As some would say, **Jabez wanted to live large for God.** It was a positive prayer. Jabez had reason to be sad and depressed. His name actually meant "sorrow," and the problems of the past were constantly on his mind. Yet he prayed a positive prayer that God heard and answered. The Prayer of Jabez is a good devotional prayer to use daily.

9. Jabez was more well-known than his brothers, because his mother named him Jabez saying, I bare him with sorrow.
*10. He was the one who prayed to the God of Israel, **Oh, that you would wonderfully bless me and help me in my work; please be with me in all that I do, and keep me from all***

harm and tragedy! *And God granted him his request.*
(1 Chronicles 4:9-10 DOT)

Daily Encounter with the Divine

Experience brings understanding. Perseverance produces victory. As one practices daily (evening and morning) devotions and prayer, they become familiar with how God works in their life. This consistent encounter with the divine prepares one for the journey ahead. Since ancient scripture was clear that the "evening and morning was the first day" it is best to begin preparation for the day the evening before. Make each day the "first day" of the rest of your life. Instead of resting from labor, now one can easily rest for their labor and begin the new morning fresh and ready to do God's work God's way.

(See Appendix A: Record of Evening and Morning Reading using The Evergreen Devotional New Testament (DNT). Order from www.gea-books. com, or order via e-mail: subesh60@gmail.com [special TT price 100TTD]

A Positive Prayer of David

David was a man after God's own heart, but he was still a man. He was a shepherd, but he went astray. Yes, he was a king, but he was still a human being. He was in the lineage of the Messiah, but he crossed the line and transgressed onto another man's territory. He had a man murdered so he could have his wife, and this brought great trouble into his life. As a troubled man, he prayed earnestly to a forgiving God as the verses below demonstrate:

How I Praise You!

*O God, my God! How I search for you! How I thirst for you in this parched and weary land where there is no water. How I long to find you! How I wish I could go into your sanctuary to see your strength and glory, for your love and kindness are better to me than life itself. **How I praise you! I will bless you as long as I live, lifting up my hands to you in prayer. At last I shall be fully satisfied; I will praise you with great joy.** (Psalms 63:1-5 TLB).*

A Constant and Consistent Prayer

The life you live day by day can make a difference in how you influence those around you. The believer's constant and consistent prayer should be, **"Lord help me to give you first place in my life every day."** We are warned that "sufficient to each day is the evil" so it is vital that the troubles and sorrows of the past not be carried over to the daylight hours. Each believer must prepare adequately before sunset for the opportunities and personal responsibilities at the sunrise. When Providence permits us to see another day, it is because there is additional accountability for the opportunities afforded. One should always remember, **"Opportunity equals obligation."** The light of a new day provides each believer both the authority to act and the responsibility to behave in a manner that uses all favorable conditions to present personal salvation to individuals and advance positive social and spiritual change.

Remember the story of the Good Samaritan where a Priest and a Levite, "each by chance," had an opportunity to serve a man in need, but did not see either the opportunity or the obligation.

A Present Weakness

Today could be a new day for each believer, the church, and the nation. Some believers are growing, reaching, and receiving; however, a lack of prayer and disciplined study of the Word seems to be a present weakness. The need is for more self-discipline and the development of a "missionary mind-set" that demands exclusive attachment to Christ with all conflicting loyalties put aside. Loyalty to the Christian cause is a consuming devotion.

The historical record on the rise of Adolph Hitler shows that he would not allow professing Christians close to him because they had a higher loyalty than allegiance to the state. This may be a negative witness, but it points clearly to the fact that no one called to be a spiritual warrior in a spiritual battle would become entangled with things that hinder the cause of Christ. If men who do not accept Christ understand the need for absolute loyalty, should believers not possess such dependability and faithfulness? Each believer must lay aside all that would hinder their full participation in God's work.

Join the Ranks

3. Join the ranks of those who share hardships as a soldier of Jesus Christ. 4. No active warrior entangles himself with ordinary affairs; so he may please the one who enlisted him as a soldier. (2 Timothy 2:3, 4 DNT)

Will you join others called of God to a new dedication, a new attitude, and a fresh commitment to self-discipline in Bible study, prayer, worship, and witness? Will you become a prayer warrior and join the battle against evil in the world? Will you become a spiritual soldier in God's army of believers? God selected you to be a vital part of His work on earth. Will you willingly accept your God-given role and become actively engaged in spiritual endeavors? There are true blessings in obedience. Seek and you will find peace in the midst of the storm of materialism and selfishness. God calls all believers to a life of disciplined prayer.

A Traditional Prayer of the Church

When a communion service was without the normal elements of bread and wine, a tradition was to pray the **Prayer of the Chalice**. This taught the people that it was not necessary to be in a formal service of worship to maintain both fellowship and a prayerful communion with God.

The Prayer of the Chalice is a personal prayer that may be used when alone or with others:

THE PRAYER OF THE CHALICE

Father, to Thee I raise my whole being
-- A vessel emptied of self. Accept, Lord this my
Emptiness and so fill me with Thyself -- Thy Light, Thy Love,
Thy Life – that these Thy precious Gifts May radiate through me
And overflow the chalice of my heart into the hearts of
All with whom I come in
Contact this day
Revealing unto
Them the
Beauty of
Thy Joy
and
Wholeness
And the Serenity of
Thy Peace which nothing can destroy.

The origin of this prayer is unknown; however, Francis Nuttall, may have been the first to shape the words in the form of a chalice.

Many Years Ago

Many years ago in an ancient land, God selected a maiden for a special responsibility: she was to be the mother of Jesus. She did not feel worthy of such an honor, and her partner was somewhat troubled by what occurred. Yet, in spite of human limitations, Mary and Joseph worked together to bring into the world a "God-child" who was to become the Savior of the world. Mary cherished her blessed event as she daily nurtured God's gift and fulfilled the daily task of raising a "child" for God. This selection and this endeavor was a benefit to the whole world. This was many, many years ago, but what about today? Has God selected you for a special task? Are you the best spouse you can be? Do you have the God given patience and skill to parent a child? Will God answer your prayers as He did in the request of Jabez? Can you actually pray and live the Prayer of the Chalice? Yes, you can, and with God's assurance you can pray, believe, and be fruitful in God's work. Always pray and believe!

"Lord, ...fill me with yourself -- your Light, your Love,
your Life – that your precious gifts may radiate
through me and overflow the chalice of my heart
into the hearts of all
with whom I come in contact
this day..."

Join with Jabez and believe!

"Oh, that you would wonderfully bless me
And help me in my work;
Please be with me in all that I do,
And keep me from all harm and tragedy!"

Pray the **Prayer of the Cross**

All through
this day, Lord,
let me touch
As many lives as possible for You. And every life I touch,
You touch them with the blessing of the Cross by the Holy
Spirit, through the words I speak,
the prayers
I pray, the
songs I sing,
the calls I
make, or my
daily life.
In the Name
Of the Christ
of Calvary.
AMEN!

Together believers can make a difference for God, here and now, in the places where God has planted each one of us. **It is not necessary to make headlines to make a difference.** God is in the quiet places and also speaks in a still small voice. Listen! As spiritual changes take place, you can make a difference in the world around you. This will include family, friends, work, church, community, and the world at large. It is great to be part of God's work done God's way! The best place to bloom is where God plants you.

Now the God of peace, that brought again our Lord Jesus from among the dead, that great shepherd of the sheep, through the blood of the everlasting covenant, make you complete in every good work to do his will, working in you that which is well pleasing in his sight, through Jesus Christ; to whom be glory forever and ever. Amen,

(Hebrews 13:20, 21 DNT).

CHAPTER TWO

BLOOM WHERE GOD PLANTS

Blessed is the man who does not walk in the counsel of the wicked or stand in the way of sinners or sit in the seat of mockers.

But his delight is in the law of the Lord, and on His law he meditates day and night.

He is like a tree planted by the streams of water, which yields its fruit in season and whose leaf does not wither. Whatever he does prospers.

Not so the wicked! They are like chaff that the wind blows away;

Therefore, the wicked will not stand in judgment, nor sinners in the assembly of the righteous.

For the Lord watches over the way of the righteous, but the way of the wicked will perish, (Psalm One).

Abide Where God Called

During World War II a Swiss Physician, A. E. Wilder-Smith, went to England to assist with the wounded. Because he spoke German, the British asked that he supervise a Prison Camp for German Officers. Food was scarce in England during the war and the prisoners had just the basic calories to keep them alive. Then one day half-loaves of bread were on the tables, and the prisoners complained about a cut in their rations. The Officer in charge responded, "Look, you have more bread than yesterday." Astonished, the obvious question came, "From where did the extra bread come?" The answer was less obvious, "The Christian families of this area decided to share their bread ration with the camp." This act of Christian kindness to a declared enemy produced a real revival, and most of the German Officers in the camp were converted. The Swiss

Doctor in charge became excited about the great faith that had spread among the Nazi Officers who were normally so unemotional that he decided after the war to abandon medicine and go into evangelism. This was a tragic mistake for the field of medicine.

An Active Witness

Becoming an active witness for Christ was not a mistake, it was where he was witnessing that was the difficulty. During the years after the war, Dr. Wilder-Smith led many to Christ during the troubling days of rebuilding Europe. However, during this time the Physician did not win a single person in the Medical Profession: no nurses, no interns, and no doctors. He became discouraged and returned to medicine and immediately began to win doctors, medical students, interns, and nurses. What was the difference? He was a Christian who practiced medicine, but when he abandoned his profession, although he was able to win a few others, he was unable to win people in the medical profession. He had failed to follow the clear words of scripture, **"Abide in the calling wherein you are called."** To put it another way, he did not "Bloom where God planted!"

> 20. Let each man **remain in the calling wherein he was called**. 21. Were you a slave when you believed, stop worrying about it: but if you are made free, live according to your calling in Christ. 22. When a man is called in the Lord being a slave, he is the Lord's freeman: likewise when one is called, being free he becomes Christ's bond-servant. 23. You were bought out of slavery; do not become the servants of men. 24. Brethren, let each **man abide with God where he is called.** (1 Corinthians 7:20-24 DNT)

Opportunity Equals Obligation

Since Genesis (1:11,12) taught us that the "seed is in the fruit," and each plant, animal, or human reproduced its own kind, we should also understand that if a Mango tree produces mangoes, or monkeys reproduce monkeys, we should be aware that God said, "Be fruitful and restock the earth." God places each of us in the "soil" where we can best grow, develop, and reproduce. In this light, a Believer should reproduce believers. How is your reproduction? It is vital for those who would serve the needs of others to look closely around where they live and work. God expects you to grow and bloom where you were planted. Do not go "some place" looking for an opportunity to serve or share; look around you for opportunity. What about family, friends, neighbors, work-mates, and the lost of your own community? Believers should never forget that **opportunity equals obligation**. Where there is need, you must fill it. Where there is hate, you must show love. Where there is hunger, you must supply food. If one is homeless you must find them a place to sleep. If one is lost you must show them the way to eternal life. To grow and bloom yourself, you must always act when and where there is a need. In fact, the best definition for evangelism is "meeting someone at their point of need." The meeting of a needy person requires action; usually this action is urgently needed. The love of Christ must be manifested without delay, and the efforts must meet the need. Seek first the Kingdom; then you will be ready to meet the needs of others.

17. For yourselves, beloved, be warned in time; do not be carried away by their impulsive errors, and lose **the firm foothold** *you have won; 18. But* **grow up in grace, and in the knowledge of our Lord and Savior Jesus Christ.** *To him be glory; now and for all eternity. Amen. (2 Peter 3:17-18 DNT)*

Burning Daylight

Since Jesus is "the Light of the World" believers should always do their work in the light. Even in the evening hours when the moon reflects the light of the sun, since Christ is with us and the Holy Spirit is always present, the work of God on earth should proceed without delay. Work now while there is light. There is an old saying used when someone was wasting time or being hesitant about their work, **"You are burning daylight!"** This admonition was used when one was dilatory or negligent about assigned tasks. In reality, they were wasting the light. The Living Bible says it well:

> 4. All of us must quickly carry out the tasks assigned us by the one who sent me, for there is **little time left** before the night falls and all work comes to an end. 5. But while I am still here in the world, **I give it my light**." (John 9:4-5 TLB)

No Artificial Light

In ancient days there was no artificial light. Fire or a lamp was used for light. During my boyhood in Plum Mitan, a village without running water or electricity, I, myself, studied by kerosene lamps and home-made flambeaux lights made from bottles filled with kerosene using pieces of burlap bags as wicks. In scripture when the word "light" is used it normally means "fire." A forerunner of Jesus was called a "burning and shining light." That means John the Baptist was on fire for God. Are you letting the fire burn in your soul so spiritual light will reflect on others? The reflected light of God is not artificial or self-generated; it is pure light sent from God through you. If the human tongue is a "fire" surely the spiritual soul can be God's true light that can light the darkness of the world through the burning soul of believers.

Reflected Light is Called "Albedo"

The moon has reflected light from the sun. Albedo literally means white, and technically, it is the rate of reflected light from a surface based on the total light falling upon that surface. For example, the earth's moon has no light of its own. What is seen is the reflected light, the albedo, of the sunlight as it is thrown back or returned toward the sun. That is what is seen from the earth. The moon absorbs much of the light and only a small part is reflected back into the atmosphere. Children have reflected light from parents, students from teachers, parishioners from religious leaders, corporations from their stakeholders, and government officials receive their power and light from the consent of the governed. How does your light shine?

Reflected Light

*33. No man who lights a lamp puts it in a closet, nor under
a box, but on a lamp stand so all may see the light. 34.
The lamp of the body is the eye: therefore when your eye
is focused your whole body has light; but when your eye is
morally bad, your body is full of darkness. 35. **Take care
that the reflected light in you does not come from moral
darkness.** 36. If you have light for the body with the absence
of darkness, the whole shall be light, as when a candle shines
brightly in the dark. (Luke 11:33-36 DNT)*

Ancient scripture informs the question that two walking
together in God's light would reflect that light on each other,
and they would share *koninea*. This word is translated **sharing,
participation, communion, and stewardship.** In reality the
concept of *koninea* points to participating in something in which
others also participate, yet the word is usually translated "fellowship." It describes a kind of mutual involvement or participation
in the light of God that is readily reflected to others. How is your
spiritual *albedo*?

Light is the Absence of Darkness

There is an old story about a man they called the
"Lamplighter." Each night in an early New England town he
would go street by street and light the gas lights at each corner.
The old gas lights were not very bright and they made only a
small light on the dark street. As the old Lamplighter went from
street to street it appeared that he was knocking holes in the
darkness. This is certainly a good example for believers. Have
you knocked any holes in the darkness in your community?

What is Missing?

The light of the sun and the moon are taken for granted.
The electricity that supplies the homes and cities with light
is an observable fact. The use of batteries to store energy
to produce light is seen as a normal part of modern life.
The occurrence of natural phenomenon such as lightning is

experienced with wonder and at time even fear. What is missing in the modern world is not "light," but the reflected light
of Christ shining through believers to a lost and darkened
world. Perhaps if we followed the injunction of Paul, to be
"on fire of the Spirit" there would be more energy for the journey and more light for the pathway. More spiritual fire would
mean more light and less darkness in the world. Remember
the two disciples walking with the Resurrected Lord on the
road to Emmaus? They asked each other "Did not our heart
burn within us, while He talked with us on the road, and as He
explained the scriptures?"

Someone the Light Shines Through

A small boy was asked by a Sunday school teacher
to describe a "saint" to the class. The boy pondered for a
moment and then said, "A saint is someone the light shines
through." A good explanation, but the surprised teacher asked,
"Where did you get that information?" The simple answer,
"I remembered the light shining through the pictures in the
stained-glass windows." Perhaps all believers should remember that children are observing God's reflected light that shines
through those professing to follow the Light of the World, Jesus.
You were, just as John, sent to witness and reflect the true
Light.

> 4. In Him was life; and that life was the light of men. 5. And
> the Light continues to shine and the darkness could not
> restrain it. 6. **God sent a man** whose name was John. **7. He
> came as a witness of the Light, that all men may accept the
> Light. 8. He was not the Light, but was sent to be a witness
> for the Light. 9. That was the true Light that came into the
> world to enlighten every man.** (John 1:4-9 DNT)

How is your Reflected Light?

Are you someone that light shines through? Do others see
Christ reflected in your life? A Christian in politics was asked
about his witness as a believer, and his answer was revealing,

"My little light shines brightly in the dark place some call politics." How is your reflected light?

It is you who are a light to the world. A town that stands on a hilltop cannot be hid. Neither does one light a lamp, and put it under a container, but on a lamp stand; and it provides light for all in the house. Likewise, **let your light shine before others so they may clearly see your good works and give glory to your Father who is in heaven.** *(Matthew 5: 14-16 DNT)*

Light, Trumpet, Shout!

In modern days we may hear "lights, camera, action," but in Judges 7, the Midianites and the Amalekites were encamped against God's people. The victory came with "lights, trumpets, and shouts!" God spoke to Gideon, and he selected a few good men to go to battle against a multitude as large as the "sands of the sea." Gideon's army took only an empty pitcher with a candle inside, a trumpet, and a testimony of faith and victory. Gideon's men encircled the enemy, smashed their pitchers to light up the night, blasted their trumpets at the same time, and shouted unison, "The Sword of the Lord and of Gideon!" The enemy was routed and killed each other or ran away. It was a great victory with only a light, a trumpet, and a victorious shout, "The Sword of the Lord and of Gideon!" It was the power of faith, the shining of light, the sounding of the trumpet, and a shout that won the victory. What could a few "burning and shining lights" in the souls of believers accomplish against the enemy with their lights shining brightly and shouts of victory, (even without a trumpet)? Even if some of us are "broken pots" God's light can still shine from us. Victory comes when we do God's work God's way.

A Little Creation History

When God created the heavens and the earth, space was made for the Garden of Eden, but there was no man to work the garden. In fact, the work was more than one person could do, so God made Adam a helpmate.

No One to Work

*5. When no plant or herb had yet sprung up in the earth, for the Lord God had not caused it to rain upon the earth and **there was no man to work** on the ground. 15. And the Lord God put the man in the Garden of Eden **to take care of it, watch and protect it, and to maintain it.** 16. And the Lord God commanded the man, saying, You may freely eat of every tree of the garden; 17. but of the tree of blessings and calamity you shall not eat, for in the day that you eat of it you shall spiritually perish. 18. Now the Lord God said, It is not satisfactory that the man should be alone; **I will make him a suitable mate**. (Genesis 2:5; 15-18 DOT)*

Adam and Eve had a wonderful chance to bloom in a sinless paradise where they were placed by God. Their failure to fulfill obligations in God's garden produced negative consequences for the whole human race. The same is true for all believers: they should be careful to flourish and blossom exactly where God puts them. In fact, scripture is clear that one should "abide in the calling where God calls." Regardless of occupation or residence, when God calls one to salvation they are expected to witness in their area of acquaintance.

A Heart of Cooperation

It takes a willing heart and cooperation to do work God's way. When it came time to construct a tabernacle to the Lord, the people gave a willing offering so the work could be accomplished. **"We have more than enough materials on hand now to complete the job!"** So Moses sent a message, **"no more donations were needed,"** (Exodus 36:4 TLB). Yet the willing heart gave more than enough, and Moses asked the people not to bring more gifts. We have not heard a similar statement in the church lately. In fact, if all members tithed and gave offerings according to their means, the work of God would be fully funded without Sunday appeals.

*29. The children of Israel brought **a willing offering** unto the LORD, **every man and woman, whose heart made them willing** to bring for all manner of work, which the LORD had commanded to be made by the hand of Moses. (Exodus 35:29 TJB)*

People Followed the Lord's Instructions

God gave instructions exactly how to build the place of worship. Following the Lord's instructions the people brought in material and gifts to provide the means to build. The workers had sufficient funds and material to complete the work. Both the workers and Moses asked that the people "stop" bringing gifts. So the work was finished following the instructions, and Moses blessed the people and declared the work was "finished" when he set up the curtain-door.

So at last Moses finished the work, *(Exodus 40:33 TLB). He finished the work because the people followed all the Lord's instructions (Exodus 39:42-43 TJB).*

Solomon's temple "was built of stone made ready before it was brought to the site," (1 Kings 5:18; 6:7). So it is with the spiritual building that believers today must construct using the materials prepared by God and constructed through cooperative efforts of many (Ephesians 2:21-22). When a work for God is started, the people must be determined to finish the project.

*28. For which of you, intending to build a lofty structure do not first estimate the cost to see if there are sufficient funds to complete the project? 29. Lest after you have made the foundation are **unable to finish** it, all those watching begin to ridicule. 30. Saying, This man began to build and was unable to finish. (Luke 14: 28-30 DNT)*

Home Comes Before Family

It appears from scripture that making preparation for a home is a precursor to establishing a family. Get the land into good order before erecting a house on it. To "build a house" may, however, be equivalent (compare Exodus 1:21; Deut 25:9; Ruth 4:11) to "founding a family," and the words are a warning against a hasty and imprudent marriage. The young man is taught to cultivate his land before he has to bear the burdens of a family. Further, in a spiritual sense, the "field" may be the man's outer common work and the "house" the dwelling-place of his higher life. He must do the former faithfully in order to attain the latter. Neglect in one is fatal to the other.

Do nothing without a plan. In winter prepare seed, implements, tackle, etc., for seed-time and harvest. 27 Finish your outdoor work and get your fields ready; after that, build your house. (Proverbs 24:27 NIV)

May the answers that I speak and the secret thoughts of my heart be acceptable to you, O Lord, my Strong Force and my Redeemer? Amen! (Psalm 19:14 DOT).

CHAPTER THREE

USE PERSONAL TALENTS

A Believer's Primary Asset

An individual may have many gifts and talents that are enhanced by education and experience, but the primary asset of a believer is **faith**, the kind of faith that comes from a confident reliance on God, His Word, and the fellowship of other believers. This faith can move mountains. It is a faith that can bring salvation and healing to lost loved ones. Faith and trust can bring an assurance of God's power to act on behalf of the needy and the unfortunate. Faith brings devotion to God and convictions by which to live. Faith that breeds loyalty and faithfulness to the Cause of Christ in the midst of a sinful world can enlarge personal talents and make them more useful to Kingdom service.

Only Faith in God

The word used for faith is *pistis* and actually means total trust and confidence coming from the sensitive side of one's nature that holds on to the belief that God keeps His promises and when His Word says something: God will do it! All believers listed in the Faith Chapter (Hebrews 11) had times of difficulty, but through a persistent faith they were able to "subdue kingdoms, produce righteousness, obtain promises, stop the mouths of lions, quench the violence of fire, and escape the edge of the sword." Each of these declarations suggests difficult situations. Only faith in God can adequately get believers through days that are "full of trouble." The starting point of obedience is "Without faith it is impossible to please God." The ultimate end of faith is "God keeps His promises!"

A Strange Story

One of the strangest stories in the Faith Chapter deals with a man named Jephthah (See Judges 11). He was illegitimate and was hated by his brothers. For a sin he did not commit, he was not allowed to inherit his father's house. His struggles caused him to become a "mighty man of valor." Typically it was those who looked down on Jephthah because of the sins of others that when trouble came and enemies were at the door, they called on Jephthah, a mighty man of war, to fight for them.

A Secret Vow

In a vow before the battle, Jephthah secretly pledged, "Give me the victory over this enemy and the first thing that comes to meet me when I return home shall be given to the Lord, or I will offer a burnt sacrifice." The first to greet him was his only child, a daughter. The Hebrew language gives a two-sided view of this vow. I side with those who believe that God would not countenance human sacrifice, and believe that Jephthah dedicated his daughter to Temple service. Had it been a young bull, he would have offered a burnt sacrifice. This view is weighted by God staying the hand of Abraham in the sacrifice of Isaac. What is the point of this strange story? There is a cost to discipleship and a price to pay for absolute trust in God. Do not make a vow lightly. Vows must be kept!

The integrity of Commitment

Does God keep His promises? A believer's steadfastness is tested when they stand on the integrity of God. This is faith that works; it is not a kind of magic that moves the hand of God. Faith is what makes a believer complete in Christ and whole as a follower of Jesus. Since God keeps His word, a believer's integrity of commitment to Christ is a bond that assures completeness. It is a firm devotion to the Word and full allegiance to principles taught in scripture. Faith comes with obedience and the root of faith is courage. The proof of faith is in the doing of it; it is the faithfulness that leads to the integrity of commitment.

Listed in the Book

You may never be listed in a book as a hero of faith. Just remember **you do not have to make headlines to make a difference** in the lives of those around you. You may feel that little has been accomplished, but God sees a different picture of you. You are His child, washed in the blood of His Son, filled with His Spirit, and walking daily by faith. You are special, and He knows the desire of your heart. Remember Joseph. He is considered by most scholars as the best type of Christ in the Old Testament. However, he was not included in the Faith Chapter (Hebrews 13) because he resisted the advances of Potiphar's wife, saved his family from starvation, saved the Land of Egypt following a great drought, or for his forgiving spirit in dealing with his brothers who sold him into slavery. He was listed in the Faith Chapter because he claimed his part of the Promised Land. God had promised to deliver His People from Egyptian bondage and return them to the land of their fathers. "By faith Joseph when he came to the end of his life, spoke of the departing of Israel from Egypt, and gave orders for the removal of his bones," (Hebrews 11:22 DNT). When Israel left Egypt they took Joseph's bones and buried them in a plot prepared by his father. The Book of Genesis begins with God's creation of the heavens and earth and ends with a coffin in Egypt, (Genesis 50:26). That was not the end of Joseph's story. Joseph's claim to fame in Hebrews was that he believed in God's promised deliverance and claimed his place in the Promise Land.

Your Talents are Useful

A pastor was preoccupied with thoughts of how to ask the congregation for more funds because church repairs were costing more than expected. He was annoyed to learn the regular organist was sick, and the last minute substitute wanted to know what songs to play. He gave her a program and said, "You'll have to think of something to play after I make the appeal for more money." During the service, he reluctantly shared the need for more funds and asked those who would pledge $500 to please stand. At that moment, the substitute organist played "Stand Up, Stand Up for Jesus." And that is how a stand-in organist became a regular! It appears her availability and talents opened a place for her. Personal talents can make a useful place for available believers. Remember, it is not ability God seeks, but availability. God has the power. Are you ready for God to work though you to build His spiritual house?

> *You yourselves are lively stones built into a spiritual house; you must be a holy priesthood to offer up spiritual sacrifices acceptable to God by Jesus Christ.* (1 Peter 2:5-8 DNT)

True Believers Share their Faith

The market-places of New Testament towns where people met to trade goods and services were a precursor to modern shopping centers. It was in such places that true believers shared a faith that worked daily. Work-place evangelism may not be politically correct, but when the Spirit draws one toward the Cross someone must witness to them concerning the saving grace of Christ. In fact, opportunity creates obligation on the part of a believer. When the door is open, or just barely cracked, it is time for the believer to act directly and decisively by presenting the gospel. Opportunity, plus personal and spiritual gifts, opens the doors of evangelism for believers. This is being faithful; it is doing God's work God's way.

God Calls Active People

Believers may support the ministry of others, but should realize that their personal talents and time are needed to produce constructive projects and programs in social and spiritual change. Active people are called to do God's work God's way. Even the temperament of a workaholic can be used to the advantage of God's work. To my knowledge, inactive or lazy individuals were not called in scripture. Leaders in the Old Testament were productive individuals whom God used to advance the cause of mankind. Early leaders in Christianity were all active and hard-working people. One was a seller of purple, another was a tent-maker, and others were fishermen, another a tax collector, but all were hard workers.

A Willing Heart

Scripture is filled with individuals who had a willingness but little else to fight against spiritual enemies. David used his bare hands to kill a lion and a bear that tried to harm his father's sheep; he used a sling and one small stone to kill Goliath and a harp to sooth the rage of Saul. Yes, David gathered five smooth stones from the brook, because Goliath had four brothers. He was prepared. Shamgar had only an ox goad, and Samson used the jaw bone of a donkey to defeat the Philistines. The young lad had only five loaves and two fishes, but Jesus multiplied the food to feed thousands. Spiritual strength and personal talent are magnified to get God's work done. What do you have to use against the enemies of the Cross? It may be small, but a willing heart is a large spiritual weapon against the force of evil.

Work Hard and Long

Hard work for the good of others never hurt anyone. In fact, those who accomplish good things work hard and long. Nehemiah was a Cup Bearer to a king when God placed on him a burden to rebuild the wall of Jerusalem. A future prophet was plowing in the field when he was called. David was a shepherd boy caring for his father's sheep when he was anointed to be the future King of Israel. God does not call lazy people to do His work. The record shows that it was a humble maiden selected to be the Mother of Jesus. A "fisherman was called to catch men" and the original disciples were busy men working to earn a living for their families when they were called to follow Jesus. It was a Greek Physician called to be St. Paul's companion and write one-fourth of the New Testament. And a well-educated Roman Jew was called to be an "apostle to the Gentiles." It was this Paul who worked as a bi-vocational minister and used his tent-making skills to support himself and others. He became a good example of hard work in both an occupation and a profession for the benefit of others.

Night and Day

*31. **Therefore be on guard and remember that for the space of three years I never stopped warning you night and day with tears.** 32. And now, brethren, I commend you to God, and to the word of his grace, which is able to make you strong, and give you an inheritance among the consecrated ones. 33. **I have never asked for silver or gold or clothing from anyone. 34. You have seen yourself that these hands have supplied not only my own needs, but for the people with me.** 35. In all things, **I gave you an example of working hard and that one must provide for the poor.** Remember the **words of the Lord** Jesus, when he said, It is more blessed to give than to receive. (Acts 20:31-35 DNT)*

Spectators or Participants

Believers must be actively involved in meeting the needs of others. To be only a watcher when there are opportunities to witness is a tragic waste of God's blessings. Some folk seem to believe the "grass is greener on the other side of the fence." It is only greener if it is watered more. One may stand and watch as the tender plants wither and die, or they could water with the Word and see new life in the kingdom. To demonstrate concern, to be fully occupied in personal witnessing is to be an active believer. Each person has the choice of being a specta-tor or a participant. Being in the spiritual game is much better than watching from the sidelines. Each person must use their personal talents and take advantage of each opportunity to participate in God's work.

Nehemiah Building the Wall

In the autobiography of Nehemiah (Chapters 1-6), some men from Jerusalem visited him, and he asked about Jerusalem. They answered, "Things are not good, the walls are still torn down and the gates were burned." When Nehemiah heard this he sat down and cried and fasted and prayed for days. He was cupbearer to the King and asked God to grant him mercy in the sight of the King.

Nehemiah had never been sad in the presence of the King, but his heart was so heavily burdened for the rebuilding of Jerusalem that the sadness showed in his face. The King asked, "Why is your face sad and you are sick at heart?" Nehemiah answered, "Why should I not be sad the city of my father lies in waste, the walls are torn down and the gates burned." And the King with his Queen asked, "What is your request?" Nehemiah asked for permission with credentials to the authorities and timber from the King's forest. The King asked, "How long will this take and when will you return?" And Nehemiah established a timeline and began the journey to do the work on the wall.

Secret Survey of the Situation

When Nehemiah arrived in Jerusalem he went secretly at night and surveyed the situation and determined what had to be done. Then he said to the people, **"Come let us build up the wall of Jerusalem that we be no more be criticized for doing something wrong."** When the people heard that the King had given permission and was to furnish the timber they said, "Let us rise up and build." And their hands were strengthened for the task at hand. When criticism came, Nehemiah said, **"The God of heaven will prosper us and his servants will rise up and build; but you who do not participate will have no portion, nor right, nor memorial in this place."**

Worked Side-by-side

And the people worked side-by-side to repair the wall and the gates of the city. Then the enemy grew angry because the wall and the gates were being rebuilt. There developed a conspiracy among the enemies to hinder the work on the wall. When the people stood up to the enemies they divided the work: half worked on the wall and half held a weapon. Then to assure a timely completion of the project each worker worked with one hand and with the other held a weapon. As they were scattered in various places working on the wall, when the enemy attacked one place, they sounded the trumpet and all the workers converged on that place to protect the work. When the enemy came strong and hid among the rubbish, Nehemiah told the people, **"Let everyone lodge in the city until the work is done."** In other words, stay at the job until it is finished.

God Blessed the Work

There will always be opposition to spiritual work. Not only is work for faith-based groups understood to be spiritual work, but the work to supply the needs of the poor is God's work. Opposition continued, and the people were about to rebel at Nehemiah's work rules because of lost wages from working on the wall. Nehemiah said, **"We will restore all you have lost. Do not worry, God is in control."** Nehemiah fed all the people at his table, and God blessed the work. It is clear that no one will lose working to rebuild what the enemy has torn down.

All but One Gate

When all was finished but one gate, the enemies called a meeting in the Plain of Ono and asked Nehemiah to come, but he said, **"OH, NO!"** Why should God's work cease while I come to your meeting? And four times the enemies tried to stop the work, but the wall was finished in fifty-two days to the glory of God and the blessing of the people. God's work done God's way will be accomplished, and the people will be blessed.

Keepers of the Gates

The Great Wall of China was built to protect the country from foreign invaders. Many years and many lives were the price of constructing the wall. In fact many workers who died on the job were buried as part of the wall itself to honor their commitment to protect their country from invaders. During many dynasties and decades the wall has stood as a symbol of concern for the safety of their country. The wall was never breached by foreign invaders, but China was invaded many times, not by breaching the wall, but **by bribing the keepers of the gates**. When all the wall of Jerusalem was completed except one gate, the enemy attempted to stop the work and leave one gate open as an easy entrance. Nehemiah, however, would not come down from the wall; he would not stop the work; and he would not go into the plain of Ono to meet with the enemy. Each time he said, **"OH NO, God's work will not be stopped until it is finished!"** Nehemiah intended to complete the wall and secure the gates. He understood that the wall not only needed gates, but strong keepers of the gates.

Strong Guards as Gate Keepers

Faith-based groups need strong guards as "Keepers of the Gates" to protect true religion from foreign elements that would contaminate the atmosphere and diminish the influence of believers. This would rob the church of power to function in the world as a true witness for Christ. Believers must earnestly strive to keep the faith pure and undefiled. As believers grow and mature they must not only contend for the purity of the faith, but they must become alert keepers of the gates. All openings in the defensive structure of the family and church must be guarded with diligent care.

Two-way Traffic

Gates provide two-way traffic. In the rigid guarding of the gates, those who peacefully enter to become a part of the culture and religion must be admitted with open arms.

However, those with hostile intent must be rejected and expelled from the gates by strong gate keepers. Also, there must be free passage out of the gate for those with the heart of a shepherd who search for the lost, the disadvantaged, the sick, or those alone, weary, and wounded on the roadside of life and desperately in need of assistance. This is true religion and what being a Christian is all about. It is not about missing hell or going to heaven: the primary concern remains reaching the lost and assisting the disadvantaged. Some who disobey will have their hell on earth, but because of Christ and the Cross, simple obedience brings blessings to those with needs and to those who willingly obey the word of the Lord.

Obedience is better than Sacrifice

All sacrificial efforts to attend church functions and go through the motions of spiritual activity will not compensate for simple obedience to the Word. The church must create an atmosphere conductive to individual involvement in outreach. It is great to pray, sing, and enjoy worship, but individuals must be both challenged to obey the call of God and sacrifice time and effort to take the saving message to the lost. It is not the corporate power of the church that reaches the lost with the gospel; it is the power of a personal testimony coming from a Spirit empowered witness.

You must remember to do good to others and give alms; God takes pleasure in the sacrifice of gifts. (Hebrews 13:6 DNT)

A Spiritual Legacy

God uses individuals to carry His message to the lost. The sanctified talents of one person can make a difference in the world. This means individuals reaching their own family, their friends, their colleagues at work, their neighbor in the community, and even their enemies. God uses the personal talents and personality of individuals to reach the lost. This sacrificial service is great, but obedience is what produces such sacrifice. An American missionary killed by natives wrote in his journal,

"A man is no fool who gives up what he cannot keep to gain what he cannot lose." To give up something you prefer for something God values is the essence of sacrifice. To submit to a missionary call is to listen to God and pay attention to a spiritual duty; it is conformity to God's will. What is done for personal advantage dies with the person, but what is accomplished for others becomes both a well spoken eulogy and a spiritual legacy.

A Well Spoken Eulogy

8. Finally, you must think the same thoughts, suffer with one another, having automatic interdependence with brotherly kindness; be tender-hearted and humble-minded: 9. you must not repay injury with injury, or hard words with hard words, but bless those who curse you. **For you were called to give kind words to others and come to a well spoken eulogy at the end**. *10. For the* **one wishing to love life and see prosperous days, let him avoid an evil tongue and cunning words. 11. Habitually avoid evil, and do good things; let him seek and follow peace.** *(1 Peter 3:8-11 DNᵀ)*

The "Fishing" Business

Peter was a fisherman and understood clearly the "fishing business," and Jesus used this personal knowledge and experience by saying, **"In the future you will use your personal talents and catch men."** Paul was a strict Jew, but also a Roman citizen and trained in Jewish Law at the feet of Gamaliel, a doctor of the law, and well educated at Tarsus in Roman arts and culture. His personal talents as a tent maker furnished much of the funds that supported his ministry. Paul also used his personal tent making business skills to provide support for others in the ministry. Jesus called farmers from the field knowing they would use their knowledge and understanding of growing things to assist the development of the pristine church. Each person has a unique contribution to the Kingdom based on their talents and work experience.

Sitting on the Premises

The congregation that sits on the premises while singing "Standing on The Promises" will certainly send the wrong message to both saint and sinner. Nero fiddled while Rome burned and now some sing and praise God, but never share their blessings with the lost world. Kingdom work needs the personal talent, time, and energy of every believer. As believers walk by faith and go about their daily lives they must share the saving knowledge of Christ with everyone who will listen; this would be doing God's work God's way.

Without a Life Changing Experience

There is no place in scripture where the lost are asked to come to a particular meeting place and sing songs they do not understand and be encouraged to participate in sacraments without a clean heart. Their personal experience is limited to attendance at meetings where they leave in the same spiritual state they were when they arrived. Leaving without a life changing experience or a burning fire in their hearts to share the good news is evidence that the local program of nurture and evangelism is not working. In fact, when a lost person enters a religious meeting still unconverted, it is evident that true believers are not following the New Testament path. The plan of the early Christians was to daily share the good news with anyone who would listen. Doing this they were encouraged by the fellowship of believers and empowered by a partnership with God.

Hear my prayer, O Lord, give ear to my humble and sincere appeal: in your faithfulness answer me. Amen!

(Psalm 143:1 DOT).

CHAPTER FOUR

PARTNERS IN FAITH

Two are Better than One

A wise man clearly understands the need for a helpmate. Many tasks cannot be completed by one individual. The assistance of others is normally welcomed. Since God made the plan that it took both male and female to produce a child, it is obvious that a child needs a two-parent family in which to grow and develop. Of course, that is the ideal, but many children grow up without the care of two parents. Whether the child is being raised by two, one, or a guardian, the best partner in any case is God. God's plan seen in human terms is a proper life-mate together with a proper home environment. When husband and wife are both believers each one has a prayer-partner. This is the ideal, but reality is that many believers do not have a spouse that is willing and able to partner with them in prayer. This becomes a hindrance to God's work done God's way. The Word is clear that "where two or three are gathered together in my Name" and when "two agree in prayer" great things happen. This is the case in childcare or any endeavor. A spiritual prayer partner is a very important asset to family life.

Reside Together as a Family

You who are husbands must be disciplined and reside together as a family, providing respectful quarters for the wife who has less strength than your own. The grace of eternal life belongs to you both, and your prayers must not suffer interruption. (1 Peter 3:7 DNT)

The Value of a Virtuous Woman

The last section of the last chapter of Proverbs (31:10-31) is a tribute to a virtuous woman with an appraised value "far above rubies." The word "virtuous" here means "characterized by moral virtue, chaste, pure, and exhibiting strength and courage." This picture is presented in twenty-two (22) two-line units, each beginning with a letter in the Hebrew alphabet in sequence in a kind of acrostic poem. It exalts the honor and dignity of women, sounds the praises of a good wife, and emphasizes the importance of the mother in the home. The secret of her dignity and honor is that she "fears the Lord," (v. 30). As a result, her husband trusts in her, and she becomes a source of honor to her whole family. It asserts that physical attractiveness is temporary, while virtue has eternal worth. This passage presents a special view of a woman of value and strength. It describes her beauty and diligence and her influence that enabled her husband to become a man with respected position and power. The tribute ends by declaring that there are many virtuous women in the world, but this particular woman, a mother viewed by Solomon, was the most excellent of them all. Baxter (1960), in his work Explore the Book, gave this virtuous woman the title "Mrs. Far-above Rubies." Search this passage (Proverbs 31:10-31), and one will find all the virtues listed below:

- **She is a good woman:**

    She works diligently

    She organizes prudently

    She behaves uprightly

- **She is a good wife:**

    She seeks husband's good

    She keeps his confidence

    She assists his prosperity

- **She is a good mother:**

    She clothes family wisely

    She feeds household well

    She gathers food sensibly

- **She is a good neighbor:**

    She helps the poor

    She uplifts the needy

    She speaks graciously

A Believing Spouse is a Gift

A believing spouse is a gift from God and should be a faith-partner. A believer must attribute worth and value to a spouse whether the spouse is a husband or a wife. Since a spouse is the "other half," there is a partnership between equals. Yet when one considers the teachings of Christianity there is a suggestion that the husband is first among equals when it comes to spiritual leadership and function. The father is expected to be the "priest" of the household, but when the father is a non-believer, the wife must assume this role.

One-half not the Better-half

Each partner is one-half not the "better half" of the relationship. This one-half is not fifty percent; each party is one whole person, and it should become a true partnership 100+100. In other words, each partner is a whole person joined with another by choice to create a home and family. When one falters, the other, who is a whole person and with God's assistance, may undertake the care and keeping of the family. With the death or absence of one, the other assumes the whole task or burden of responsibility. Yet, scripture and the macho society seem to devalue the female and attempt to present her in a subservient or submissive role. Based on the physiological nature of gender rather than the correct God assigned value, one becomes preoccupied with the stereo-typical function rather than the true worth of a spouse. With believers this is easily corrected by scripture, "In Christ there is neither male nor female." Yet there are different gender func-tions and roles that are obvious. Femininity and masculinity are both observable and valued in society and must be appreciated in faith-based arenas.

The man who finds a wife finds a good thing; she is a blessing to him from the Lord. (Proverbs 18:22 TLB)

An Unbelieving Spouse

A tragedy of the modern faith-based environment is that many good men and women do not have a believing spouse. This does not mean that such individual believers are excluded from sharing their faith both inside and outside the home. If the unbelieving spouse desires to remain in the marriage and agrees to refrain from sexual contact outside of marriage, the believer may remain and maintain an active faith and witness. Although it is a hindrance when a believer does not have a prayer-partner in the home, this does not exclude them from the basic work of a believer. Yet, each believer needs a prayer-partner and should consult with spiritual leaders as to an individual in the church who would fill this gap. Surely the ladies' prayer band or the men's fellowship has individuals willing to join with a believer who is without a prayer-partner. In such case, the believer should discuss the matter with their spouse and explain that not having a prayer-partner was a spiritual disadvantage and share the process of seeking a partner for prayer. It is best that the unbelieving spouse know and understand who and why a prayer **"only"** partner is needed.

It is also good for the unbelieving spouse to understand that their lack of faith and/or faithfulness may become a hindrance to the spiritual development of the children. Yet, scripture is clear that the believing spouse must be assured that the partner is totally and completely separated from immorality to maintain a wholesome home environment and not unduly penalize the children by their exposure to unfaithfulness and betrayal. It is extremely difficult to bring a child into Christianity when one of the parents remains an unbeliever.

*12. But to the rest I speak, not the Lord: If a brother has an unbelieving wife and she is pleased to reside with him, let him not send her away. 13. And the woman who has an unbelieving husband who is pleased to reside with her, let her not leave him. 14. **For the unbelieving husband is separated from immorality by the wife, and the unbelieving wife is separated from immorality by the husband: else their children would be defiled;***   *(1 Corinthians 7:12-14 DNT)*

A Perspective on the Spiritual Family

When it becomes clear that a spouse is a gift from God there is a different evaluation and perspective on the spiritual nature of family. Scripture is clear that there is one *laos* (laity or the people of God). There is no upper class, no big I," or little" you." Clergy, elders, deacons, and other leadership roles are simply recognized functions in the church. This does not mean that the leaders are a better class of Christians. God is no respecter of persons. The requirements for salvation and Christian service are the same for all. One is not loved more or saved better and then moved into a higher category. However, different people are recognized as having an elevated func-tion in the church. All are the same from God's perspective. There is one Lord, one Faith, one Baptism, and one People of God. There are no significant differences in the salvation or spirituality of those who function in specific roles. God expects all the "people of God" to live clean, pure lives separated from immorality. This is not a standard just for those who function in leadership; it is a customary expectat on of all who claim redemption through Christ.

Shared Equality and Value

Each person in the Body of Christ shares equality and value. A General of the Army is still a soldier. A pastor (shep-herd) is still a sheep. A deacon is still a member of the local church. The highest leaders in Christianity remain a part of the laity. A rule of leadership is that no one should be asked to do anything that the leader would not do. If the leader asks the membership to witness and share their faith in their daily lives, is the leader not also obligated to do the same? The concept of "leadership" suggests that those functioning as leaders are "out in front" and are good examples of both attitude and action. The greatest preacher in the land is not effective with-out daily involvement in personal witness demonstrated by a lifestyle that recommends Christ to the world. A leader by atti-tude and action must influence others to follow and participate in the outreach ministry of a faith-based group.

To be Called Christian

When the "disciples were first called Christians" in Antioch, the words "were called" meant "to transact business, or to be employed in accomplishing something." After one whole year of discipleship training by Paul and Barnabas, converts began to transact their affairs as Christians in Antioch, (Acts 11:26). At first this was a lifestyle recognized by the business community of Antioch. It was not a derogatory term; it was an obvious recognition of a change in the behavior of believers. The first use of "Christian" as a behavior was honorific in nature; it was a compliment directed at the change in the way the believers engaged in daily contact with the community. Later the term "Christian" became a mark of identification as a follower of Christ, but a positive lifestyle was strongly implied by the classification as being a "follower of Christ." Sadly, many who are called Christian do not live a life worthy of the name. They are nominal Christians or in name only and become a negative influence on others. Paul used the word "wasted" in speaking of the days when he did not actively support the church. This word "wasted" is the opposite of "building up;" in fact, if one is not supporting Christianity by a witnessing lifestyle they are indeed "wasting their connection" and are doing great harm to God's work.

Business is a Venture

A business is a venture or risk on the part of the stakeholders, but for the public it must be dependable as a fixed asset with an air of permanency. The business of business must be relevant and relational. A business is an organization, and therefore, the principles that work in business also work in an organized faith-based group. In fact, shepherd management and servant leadership used in the church also works in business. Since this is true, believers have a great deal to offer business, and the church should listen to those who operate a business. Management concerns the whole of the organization while leadership relates to the needs and welfare of individuals within the organization. All believers must be "apt" or ready to teach and willing to be out front as a leader showing others the way to genuine discipleship and witness.

Keys to a Business Plan

Believers in business are in business with God. The standard key to progress is a comprehensive overview of the business idea. It outlines what the business will do and how it will be launched, covering everything from funding to dealing with competitors. What market need will it satisfy? The following eight keys help unlock the secret of a prosperous business when the keys are used in faith. You may add more.

- Detail the ideas that would attract potential partners.

- Provide the framework for what the business is about.

- Identify the target market and its needs.

- Isolate a possible competitive edge.

- Name the service/product to be produced or marketed.

- Describe the day-to-day operation.

- Pinpoint expected income and cash flow.

- Name the leadership team.

Main Entrance

Once there was a small business operated by a wise man. His store was between two large ones who advertized their merchandise and had big sales. The small owner had only one sign, which he erected over his door when the other two stores had big sales. The sign "**Main Entrance**" was placed over his front door, and the public often thought his door was the main entrance to the big sales. Finally, the owner of one of the big stores purchased the little store, and the small business owner retired in comfort. Perhaps if you can't beat them; buy them out. Although this "gimmick" worked as an attention-grabber for this small business, normally, ethical businessmen do not utilize such tricks.

Honest Business

All who would do honest business must keep their promises because "your word is your bond." Dependability is the proper word. It is a similar concept as the one used to describe a reliable and trustworthy man in scripture, "And I will fasten him as a nail in a sure place," (Isaiah 22:23). This was leadership with fixed permanent dependability. What does it mean to be a relevant business related to the community, appropriately structured, with useable and applicable products, and that is important or even significant as a leader? A business is not a leader just because it was first, but because among others it stands out as a "brand." When that "brand" denotes a spiritual commitment, the business becomes a partner with God in kingdom work.

Scripture appears to be Masculine

The ancient world was a totally masculine environment. The language, the customs, and all the traditions pointed to a "man's world." For example, in ancient China, many years before Christ, the pictorial script of the Chinese language used for "women/wife" was a picture of a man and a horse. When asked for an explanation, a scholar from China explained the ancient world saw a woman as a **"man who works like a horse."** It was in this masculine world that Christianity began. This is the explanation for the maleness of scripture; it does not mean that women are second class in the scripture. It was just the culture. This was corrected by New Testament scriptural recording, "In Christ there is neither male nor female" and further clarified by, "God is not a respecter of persons." When one behaves in a positive manner and their lifestyle speaks of honesty and fairness, they become relational. What does it mean to be relational? It means to behave as family, feel friendly and behave as the next of kin. If you are a believer then you become related to other believers, and gender is not an issue.

Masculine Leadership

Based on an understanding of Holy Scripture, even the New Testament, the Bible appears to be a masculine book. This may seem unfair in the light of modern politically correctness; however, there is a true message in the masculine leadership in spiritual matters. Since the Garden of Eden, the wife has been seen as not only a helpmate, but an equal partner. Some men see this as an inferior or lesser position for the female, but it is a God-given place of service. It simply means that there is a plan for both to be involved in God's work. The roles may be different, but they are equally important. They are both soldiers in the Army of the Saints. The female is the glue that holds society together. The wife is the key to the morality of the family. Women have unique and special roles in community activities, and in modern times, often leadership roles in government and industry. Women must not be denied their place as a useful and working partner in God's work. Yet, women must not permit their gender to become a stumbling stone to others.

The Home Front

In the last days the Bible speaks about wars and rumors of wars. History reveals that in time of war an individual soldier, normally male, goes off to fight the enemy. While one goes to the "front lines" and perhaps in harm's way, it takes several individuals on the home front to support that one warrior on the battlefield. This may be the case with many of the praying spouses, sisters, mothers, grandmothers, aunts, and cousins within an extended family who prayerfully support a spiritual soldier in the Army of the Saints. While the men may be up front leading the charge, their wives and other prayer warriors are supporting and protecting the home front and providing the moral support that gives the men the character and courage to lead. This does not diminish either role; they are a team, and each has a vital role in the family, the spiritual worship, and the outreach to the community. Perhaps it is as the old saying, **"The man may be the head, but the wife is the neck that turns the head and points it in the right direction."** What is not observed is that when God places a woman in a leadership position it is usually because some man has failed to assume their proper duties. When God looks for a man to "stand in the gap" and does not find one, a godly woman may be chosen to do the work.

Submit is not a Negative Construct

Spiritual submission is a God-given awareness of the worth and value of a spouse. The idea that husband and wife should "submit" to each other embraces the reality that marriage changes personal arrangements. The concept of "submit" is not a negative construct; it simply means **"to line up under the authority (name) of another."** As a single person the spouse was under the authority (name) and guidance of parents. Once married, life was rearranged, reorganized, reprioritized, and sometimes revitalized in a different arena where their roles and function became the moral force for a new and growing family. The importance of a spouse and particularly a parent should never be devalued. The arms that hold the baby has the mind and hands that literally rule the world. Those who neglect or diminish the role of husband, wife, father, or mother become the casualties of the moral and spiritual battles that confront both family values and spiritual growth for all concerned. Not only must there be the attitude of submission to one another, but there must be submission to God and His plan for the family, the church, and the outreach ministry of believers. When believers submit to God they line up under His authority (name). This spiritual submission makes the "submit" connected with marriage more understandable and pleasant.

Submit is a Two-way Street

It should be clear that husbands also must line up under new arrangements. Once he had only himself to support, now the spouse and perhaps soon a child are his growing responsibility. Living quarters must be larger, more food is required, and a larger-automobile may be needed. Expenses grow as the family grows. The construct of "submit" is a two-way street. The arrangements, responsibilities, and accountabilities are different for both husband and wife, but it is clearly a two-way street in which the family should function as a mutual admiration society. This is God's plan for the family and the way to develop a spiritual team to do God's work. This may require a change of mindset for some.

A Change of Mindset

The rearrangement included leaving their present home and family and moving to different quarters with a spouse. The relocation required a change of mindset, attitude, and a total reorganization of living arrangements. The adjustments to the new living conditions produce a restructuring of both the present and the future and essentially reprioritized life. The main concern is now the spouse and their future family. Functioning physically and personally in this different arena brings an understanding of God's plan for the family. This reality brings refreshment and rejuvenation. This new role includes not only caring for a spouse and the children, but also the creation of a positive environment in which the family lives and grows.

Transformation of Arrangements

The community, school, and church take on new and different importance as couples begin to function as companions and caregivers for the family. Producing a child brings a great transformation of arrangements and a new perspective on life and living. Both husband and wife now realize that they can be personally productive with several multitasking skills, and this brings a revitalized understanding of each individual's role in life. A spouse is a gift from God to the family, the church, and to a larger extent to the whole community. In fact, the supreme example of marriage is "Christ and the Church." Scripture teaches that the "Church" is the Bride of Christ. When marriage is a spiritual union, the couple becomes the anchor of the whole society. Those who underestimate the role and value of husband and wife do so at their own peril and present great danger to society as a whole.

Moral and Spiritual Values

As confidence and trust develop between husband and wife, the assurance of marriage faithfulness and commitment increases and the cause of Christ is blessed. This produces a dedication to moral and spiritual values for the family, the church, and the community. A devotion to things spiritual creates an involvement in the building of community and the outreach of the gospel. The family home becomes an extended sanctuary for growing children, spiritual development, and disciple-making. Husband and wife plus the first child meet the requirement for worship, "where two or three are gathered together Christ will be found in their presence," and the true church happens. The home must become the center of moral and spiritual values, and these virtues should radiate out from the family altar in the true spiritual sanctuary of the home. This is truly doing God's work God's way.

True Partnership

To see a spouse as a gift from God is necessary to develop a partnership in God's work. **"Can two walk together except they agree?"** True partnership with one's life-mate is a prerequisite to spiritual involvement in doing God's work. It is this "true and faithful partnership" that supplies the grace, encouragement, and support required to be involved in disciple-making, spiritual growth, family leadership, and a positive influence on faith-based groups and the community at large. It is the true partnership that makes things happen for the good.

Good Families make Good Churches

In reality, the church does not make good families; it is good families that made good churches. When the early church was being initiated, the rule was to seek out married men with good children, a good reputation in the community, who were not greedy after material things. It was these men who built the stable families that established good churches in the New Testament. It is still the case today. Churches do not build good families. Good parents establish good families, and these good families make a good church and expand the Kingdom. The family becomes the key that unlocks access to spiritual progress. When there is a lack of progress in spiritual matters, the state of marriage should be the first place examined. As marriage goes, so goes the local church and the community. Without the model of affection and consideration given in the marriage arrangements, the church and ultimately Christianity suffers a near fatal blow.

Need for Good Role Models

It was not a professional minister or a spiritual leader who brought to the attention of the world the need for good role models and good examples. It was William Shakespeare in Early English society who called attention to those who had strong guidelines for others, but did not follow their own rules. He expressed concerns about the behavior of parents and moral leaders who had become **"good bad examples"** to the young. Although much of his literature is hard to understand, it appears that Shakespeare clearly understood the human element that can **intrude, interfere, and interrupt** human communication and hinder moral leaderships in the family and society. Shakespeare was also aware of faith-based individuals who did not live up to their own standards. The enemy uses any crack or opening in a Christian's armor against the whole cause of Christ. All who choose to walk the path that leads to life eternal or decide to lead in Christianity must **"hold fast to that which is good"** and become a good example of believers to all concerned elements of society. When the mighty fall the other warriors flee. This is the tragic result of moral and ethical failure by believers.

The Noble Task of Spiritual Leadership

Working as full physical and spiritual partners in the endeavor called "family," a spouse becomes a mentor, life-coach, guidance counselor, and a disciple-maker. Each partner becomes a true life-mate and work-mate to their spouse and a vital force for moral excellence in the community and the church. Marriage is a sacred union of two individuals with special abilities and qualities that together create the nucleus of a family. Those who take marriage vows are brought into the closest and most sacred of human relationships. Their lives are blended as the waters of two confluent streams and share both the joys and sorrows of life. From marriage unions spring all the sweet charities of family and home and all the refining virtues that flow out from this sacred and cherished intimacy. The family group is truly a God-made spiritual arrangement that reproduces others with functional roles in God's work.

The Family Enterprise

Since marriage is a partnership and each member is a vital part of the family enterprise, it is by example that the spouse leads in their respective roles and becomes equal spiritual partners. Husbands must be aware that in many aspects of modern culture, women are given vital leadership roles in the community and the church. Society is strengthened by the attitude and action of women, provided they do not neglect their primary role of wife and caregiver of children. The maternal nature of the feminine character can well provide a nurturing benefit to all aspects of life and community. The family, the community, the church, and the Nation as a whole can be developed and nurtured by the wives and mothers of the land. The loving and moral character of the senior women in the network of the family and the church can provide vital influence on the nature and development of the Nation. Also, the wife must never diminish the God-given role of her partner.

*1. This is a faithful saying, if a man desire leadership oversight, he is aspiring to a noble task. 2. One holding an office of watchful care must be scrupulous, faithful to one wife, watchful, sensible, orderly, hospitable, experienced in teaching; 3. Neither intemperate, nor quarrelsome, free from the love of money; but gentle, not contentious, not a craving for possessions; 4. **he must be one who is a good head of his own family, and keeps his children in order by winning their full respect; 5. if a man has not learned how to manage his own household, will he know how to govern God's church?** 6. Not a recent convert lest being puffed up fall into judgment of the devil. 7. Moreover he must have a good report from those outside the church; that he not fall into reproach and into the snare of the devil. (1 Timothy 3:1-7 DNT)*

Present Tense Qualifications

All who would evaluate or judge candidates for leadership roles should remember the scriptural standard is presented in the present tense. Should one view the past of most individuals, no one would be qualified for leadership; however, the Holy Spirit was careful to guide the hand of Paul to place the qualifications in the present tense. The past is forgiven; it is under the blood and should not be remembered against an individual when they have made things right with God. When God forgives, the Church must forgive. There was only one perfect man: the man Christ Jesus. If Satan damaged your life in the past, and it is now under the blood of Christ, just hold your head up high and "March" with the redeemed ones. All believers are created equal. When one is washed in the blood of Jesus they are regenerated, redeemed, and ready for full-time Christian service. Regardless of how one may earn a living, the function of being a Christian is full-time, everyday, all the way from the altar to the grave to the door that opens to eternal life.

Standards for Spiritual Partners

All kingdom workers have similar qualifications for holding an office or functioning in a particular role in relation to the Christian cause. They may appear to be worded a little differently, but basically they are the same. God does not require more of one believer than of another. It is just that the church should evaluate candidates for positions based on a written standard.

> *8. In the same way leaders must be serious, sincere in their talk, not addicted to wine, not craving wealth; 9.* **keeping true, in all honesty of conscience, to the faith that has been revealed.** *10. And let the ministers first be tested and undergo probation; then being found without accusation, let them function as a minister. 11.* **Even so must their wives be grave, not slanderous gossipers, temperate, faithful in all things.** *12. Let the ministers be a man married to one woman, and manage their own children and household well. 13.* **For those who have ministered well acquire for themselves a good position and fluency of speech of the faith founded on Christ Jesus.** *14. I am writing these things hoping to come to you shortly; 15. but if I am delayed* **that you may know how you should conduct yourself in the family of God, which is the assembly of the living God, and the pillar and bulwark of the truth.** *(1 Timothy 3:8-15 DNT)*

Defeating Selfishness

Self-centeredness and self-interest are two blights on any relationship. Love is really directing interest and value toward one's mate, but when selfishness turns a person to selfish acts, the relationship is in trouble. True love brings a self-sacrifice that may require the giving up of personal wants and even needs for the benefit of a partner. **Unless selfishness is defeated, the relationship is doomed.** A couple can survive in the same ship as long as it is not a battleship. It may not be the "love boat," but provided the boat is a simple canoe for two, both must paddle in the same direction usually upstream and not just drift with the current. Paddling in different directions or drifting with the flow of the stream will eventually lead to either the treacherous rapids or a dangerous waterfall. Those who would defeat selfishness must persevere and be steadfast of purpose in all aspects of life. A true love relationship prompts one to abandon personal wants for the benefit of a spouse or family member. There is no place for selfishness in a Christian family or any spiritual endeavor. Partners should become good friends, true companions, and honest colleagues. This makes them good examples to all concerned.

Without the Institution of Marriage

Marriage is basically a partnership. The Hebrew text (Proverbs 18:22) teaches a general principle, **"He that finds a wife finds a good thing."** St. Paul adds, "Marriage is honorable in all." Had the world been left without the institution of marriage as a moral safeguard to corral the unbridled immoral inclinations, civilization probably would not have developed as we know it. Scholars, who want to add to the Hebrew text the word "good" as a modifier of wife, forget that most wives were good in the first place and deteriorated living with a defective husband. The facts are clear: there are good and bad spouses and sufficient faults and blame on both sides of the gender gap for any disturbance or any pattern of activity or behavior that brings dysfunction in a marriage relationship. It is clear that a bad marriage can limit an individual's influence in many aspects of life and create an environment where both husband and wife become weak links in the chain of disciple-making and poor examples of moral and social stability to their family and the community.

Singleness is Commendable

Marriage is honorable, but singleness is commendable. The ability to remain unmarried in the modern world is an admirable gift. Paul said it is good for one to remain in a state of singleness, provided their life is dedicated to the Lord. In such cases there is an advantage to singleness because "the unmarried woman cares for the things of the Lord, that she may be holy both in body and in spirit." Then Paul added that a single person "may attend upon the Lord without distraction."

Finally, Paul made it clear that even a widow who was free to marry would be happier if she remained single. This in no way was meant to disparage marriage, but points out Paul's sense of nearness of the coming of the Lord and the need not to be distracted. As Shakespeare wrote, "To be or not to be, that is the question." The choice remains one for each individual. *(See 1 Corinthians 7:8, 34, 35, 39, 40.)*

Foundation Stones of Partnership

One should clearly understand the foundation stones of a marriage partnership. Those stones are **accountability, responsibility, and trust.** To be a functioning party in a contract, one must grasp the responsibilities and obligations with reference to the contracted relationship. The stable marriage relationship is the basic unit of a moral society and the essential element in a functioning place of worship. Without the foundational relationship in the marriage union that cultivates accountability, responsibility and trust there will be no strong and vibrant faith-based worship. The relationship of husband and wife is compared with the connection between Christ and the Church. The stable marriage relationship then becomes the foundation stones for a moral society and a ministering church.

The relationship between Christ and the Church is a model for the behavior of husband and wife. Since there are failures on the part of the church toward Christ, there will be failures in the marriage relationship. Yet, there is redemption and restoration when both parties agree to make the necessary change to bring reconciliation to the relationship.

Compromise and Contract

Relationships are based on an agreed contract that requires a compromise. Originally, **com - promise** was a mutual promise coming from the word "com"- **together with** and **"to promise."** The parties agreed to adjust and settle a difference by mutual consent, with concession on both sides and to surrender one's own self-interest to gain a benefit. In a spiritual sense this is the ministry of reconciliation. This requires both parties to establish social contact and mutually agree to promise together that each will give up something to achieve something better.

They must agree to disagree agreeably. This requires either a written or spoken agreement that is in reality a contract that reduces the tension, narrows the differences, and expands the possibilities of the relationship. To create a true partnership in Christ, such understanding and agreements are necessary. Love alone is not sufficient to hold a relationship together; the human element always puts a "fly in the ointment." Such a mutual agreement requires both partners to constantly repair and regularly mend any broken fences, and at times nurture the healing of a broken heart. When this occurs, marriage becomes a productive union blessed by Providence, and the Christian cause is advanced. Marriage may not be perfect, but it is much better than the alternative for most believers.

Contract vs. Covenant Marriage

A covenant marriage is legally distinct from the more common contract marriage. Contract requires only licenses and solemnization, while covenant marriage requires premarital counseling and limited grounds for divorce. Some are choosing "covenant" over "contract" for the content of marriage vows. The covenant issues came to being to improve traditional values relating to the marriage relationship. It is also assumed that the inclusion of covenant issues in the legal process has influenced the elements of a stable marriage relationship.

The covenant approach to marriage was initiated because of the limited rules that permit easy marriage and easy divorce. Divorce and cohabitation have increased in the past four decades. Women and children are the big losers; however, data suggest that men have also become losers. It appears that divorce brings health issues, greater financial problems, moral and spiritual concerns to the men involved. This does not take into account the damage done to the males in breaking promises, and their limited influence on their children.

Marriage is a Blessing

Notwithstanding all its dysfunction and embarrassments, the marriage relationship is a blessing. In most cases, a soulmate is better than being alone, because celibacy is normally considered to be abnormal and requires a consecration that most are unwilling or unable to make, especially in this present sensually charged, self-indulgent society. At creation it was clearly stated, **"It is not good for man to be alone."** St. Paul made it clear to the early church that it was better to marry that to attempt to contain the passions of the flesh. Marriage can be a blessing that brings morality and stability to individuals, the family, and the community. A stable marriage also becomes a blessing to the church because it opens many doors of opportunity to both men and women to be involved in building a moral society. Marriage also enables a meaningful worship experience and a team approach to growing good families, good churches, and a productive outreach and disciple-making venture that is compatible with Holy Scripture and positive social and spiritual change.

So may the grace of the Lord Jesus be with God's people.
Amen.
(Revelation 22:21 DNT).

CHAPTER FIVE

POSITIVE SOCIAL CHANGE

The Cooperative Efforts of Many

When God looked at Adam in the Garden, the divine understanding was, "It is not good for man to be alone." This brought about the need for an suitable "helpmate." It is clear from this and all of history that everyone needs the friendship and assistance of others to accomplish anything worth human effort. God places individuals together not only to help each other but to work together for the good of others. Unless one lives a life larger than their self interest, they will never be comfortable working together with God and others to meet the greatest needs of mankind. Positive social change will come only through the cooperative efforts of many. This requires a networking of believers.

Networking for Positive Change

Most communities are too large for only a few to meet the growing needs of people. Believers should endeavor to make contact with as many individuals as they can to assist their cause either through volunteer labor or the provision of funds. The exchange of ideas between various individuals and groups located in a community can open the doors of opportunity to serve. As associations are built and people begin to act together for a common cause, great strides can be made in positive social change. The task of serving the greater needs of a community multiplies as time passes. The sooner corrective or preventive action takes place the easier it is to make a difference and push individuals and families toward positive change. Some have said that, "it takes a village to raise a child." Well, it takes cooperative effort, lots of energy, a few dollars, and persistence to work together and make a difference in a family or a community. Networking then becomes the process or practice of building relationships among people who could bring advantages or opportunities to a cause.

Thinking Alone not Sufficient

It seems a family was driving on the main road and came upon an old homemade camper. On the back of this crudely made vehicle was a sign that read, "Slow down you have caught up with the Joneses." Upon reading the sign the driver said, "I always thought when I caught up with the Joneses they would refinance, and I would still be behind." This suggests that thinking about funds or the future is not sufficient to change things; in fact, only hard work will produce positive future change. The old saying, "Prayer changes things" is incomplete. What really takes place is that people are changed through prayer and then changed people change things. Normally, working alone is not enough, prayer and labor networking with like-minded people is necessary to assure positive change and spiritual progress.

Believers Must Network

From the earliest days of Christianity, believers have gathered together in small groups for fellowship and worship. Whether it was a prayer meeting in the home of John Mark led by his mother, or a prayer meeting by the river conducted by a woman who sold purple, or in an upper room with Jesus and His disciples, believers have gathered in groups. One warning of the New Testament was clear, as the last days come, believers must not neglect the gathering together for prayer, praise, and worship. This gathering together was a kind of spiritual network that strengthened the early believers. Networking for worship and joining together to unite for worthy projects is still doing God's work God's way.

*22. Let us come forward with a sincere heart crammed full of faith, having our guilty consciences purified by sprinkling, and our bodies washed with pure water: 23. Let us not waver in acknowledging the faith we profess; we have a promise from one who is true to His word. 24. Let us keep one another in mind, always ready with love and acts of piety, 25. **Let us not abandon our meeting together**, as*

some habitually do, but let us encourage one another, and all the
more as we see the great day drawing near.
(Hebrews 10:22-25 DNT)

One Accord in One Place

There is no substitute for the force created by being in one accord, in one place, to do God's work. Scripture is clear that those who walk with us on a spiritual journey can be a source of encouragement. Where a few (two or three) are united for a cause, the presence and strength of Christ is joined to the work. Knowing this, believers should always give God the credit for all achievements in their work together. Even Adam was not left alone in the garden; he was given a helpmate by God. Do not attempt God's work alone; everyone needs the strength that comes from the support of others. There is an old story of a man who had several sons, and he wanted to teach them the value of working together. He gathered up a number of sticks and bundled them and asked the youngest to break the bundle. He could not. Then the father went up the line to the eldest who could not break the bundle of sticks. The father then took the bundle apart and handed each son a stick and said, "Break it!" They quickly learned the strength of being together. Teamwork and partnership is the key to positive social and spiritual change.

Teamwork and Partnering

When some people think of network they assume it is socializing with men and women in fancy suits, polite conversation, and the exchanging of business cards, but I see social and business networking as a spiritual process of sharing a vision and a cause with people who are concerned about others and have a sense of compassion for the less fortunate in society. I see networking as an interesting experience with people who are socially responsible and accountable to themselves for the support of a worthy cause. When two or three get together for a good work they are automatically joined by the Spirit of Christ.

Therefore, I see the process of working together with others for the common good as teamwork and a partnering with God in caring for the needs of others.

Focused Networking

Networking must be focused and guided by sincere motives. The objective is not to take advantage of anyone, but rather to provide others an opportunity to join the cause, share in the mission, and develop support for a worthy project. Making a connection with other individuals who may share your vision for a particular cause and perhaps will share in supporting the cause with energy and effort is an exciting adventure. When people join together much can be accomplished. When the people of the earth decided they could build a city with a tower whose "top may reach even unto heaven" (*Geneses 11: 1-9*), God saw the unity of the people and scripture records "now nothing will be restrained from them." As long as they were in agreement and understood each other they were able to complete whatever project they started. The lesson here is clear: unity is the route to achievement, and confusion is the path to failure.

Networking Rules

1. Networking is taking advantage of each opportunity to associate with others who may share my vision and who may be interested in and support projects or programs that advance the general mission.

2. Networking is being approachable and being friendly with those who may be interested in supporting the cause I want to advance.

3. Networking is about ideas, values, and interests. It is gathering individuals who share a common desire to advance a particular mission or cause. It is about shared passion and shared opportunities to participate in a worthy cause or project.

4. Networking means spending a significant amount of time engaging people and sharing with them my passion for a particular cause.

5. Networking is best accomplished in meeting people face to face. The Internet or other electronic technology may be used to establish initial contact, but networking requires personal contact. People want to see my personal passion for the cause. This often does not come through in alternative means of communication. Personal, face to face contact is the key to networking.

6. Networking is establishing and maintaining a relationship with others who share a common vision. When others see the concern and passion we share, they will catch the vision and assist the mission.

7. Networking is teamwork and partnering with others to pass on information and to share in advancing a common cause for the common good.

God Oversees the Spiritual Work

From a Heavenly Throne God oversees the spiritual work of believers involved in the task of carrying the gospel to the four corners of the earth. God is Spirit and uses the mind and body of believers to do spiritual work on earth. Believers must become workers together with God to accomplish the basic commission of Christ. With the enabling of the Holy Spirit, believers become the hands that do the work, the feet that carry the gospel, the ears that hear the cries of the needy, and the eyes that see the urgency of action required to accomplish God's work. Meeting these needs becomes part of a spiritual commission to share in the Kingdom's work. God furnishes the power to act but leaves the decision to act to believers. Paul saw believers as an "open letter from Christ" written in their hearts ready to be read by all. The lives of all believers are an open book that tells the world both the good and the bad about our attitude, action, and lifestyle. This determines the value of our Christian witness.

> *2. You are our letter of recommendation written in our hearts, known and read of all men: 3.* **you are an open letter from Christ transcribed by us,** *written not with ink, but with the Spirit of the living God; not on tables of stone, but on pages of the human heart. (2 Corinthians 3:2, 3 DNT)*

God leaves a lot for Human Hands

A proud farmer was bragging about his flourishing crop when a visitor confronted his arrogance, "You should give God the credit for this crop because he supplied the land, the sunshine, the minerals, and the rain." The farmer responded, "You should have seen that field when God had it by Himself. He sure left a lot of work for me and the boys!" It is true that God furnishes all the necessary elements for a good harvest, but God does not do the plowing, the sowing, the weeding, or the gathering of the harvest. Although God is working, he leaves a lot for human hands to do. Wise believers do not frustrate the will of God; they work together with God and much is accomplished. An old poem by Annie Johnston Flint speaks to this issue of God using believers to do His work:

Christ has no Hands but our Hands to do His Work Today!

He has no feet but our feet to lead men in the way
He has no tongue but our tongue to tell men how He died
He has no help but our help to bring them to His side.

We are the only Bible the careless world will read,
We are the sinner's gospel; we are the scoffer's creed;
We are the Lord's last message, given in word and deed;
What if the type is crooked? What if the print is blurred?
What if our hands are busy with other work than His?

What if our feet are walking where sin's allurement is?
What if our tongue is speaking of things His lips would spurn?
How can we hope to help Him or welcome His return?

Working Together With God

God and men work together in the process of making disciples. God is willing to bless the efforts of human hands; in fact, there can be no harvest without the touch of the Master's hand. To grow a vegetable garden there must be diligent cultivation, careful, hopeful planting, unceasing effort, constant prayerful attention, and saintly patience. The crop must then be touched by the hand of God to grow. Scripture is clear: one plants, another waters, but God gives the harvest. Believers must work together with God to assure spiritual progress. Paul understood the cooperative process of working together with God and wrote:

*6. I did the planting, Apollos watered; but **God caused the growth**. 7. So neither the planter nor the one doing the watering deserves credit, but God who gave the growth. 8. Now he who did the planting and the one doing the watering are part of the same process: and every man will receive a reward according to his work. 9. **For God is working and the laborers are together: you are God's farm, you are God's field to be worked and God's building to be constructed**. 10. According to the favor of God given to me, as a wise master builder, I have laid a foundation, and another will build on it. **But let every worker take heed how he builds on the foundation.** (1 Corinthians 3:6-10 DNT)*

Cooperation with God's Plans

Doing God's work God's way requires cooperation with God's plans. The Father did His part and sent Jesus. The Son did His part and sacrificed His life on Calvary's Cross and gave the early disciples a commission to make other disciples as they went everywhere witnessing of the saving Grace. The Holy Spirit is presently doing His work of making us aware of both the sins of omission and the overt wrongdoings. Also, the Spirit reminds us that there will be a day of reckoning when all will give account for their action or their failure to act when there was an obvious opportunity.

*13. For everyone who calls upon the name of the Lord shall be saved. 14. **How shall they call on him in whom they have not learned to believe? And how shall they believe in him of whom they have never heard? And how shall they hear without a messenger? 15. And how shall they proclaim, except they be sent?** (Romans 10:13-16 DNT)*

Subsidiary Tenants

God made the world, and the human race became subsidiary tenants with instructions to care for the earth and all living things and to be "fruitful." Jesus was given the task of redeeming the world after the sin entered the Garden. This was done by many years of preparation under the Law of the Old Testament that became a schoolmaster bringing the human race to Christ. This was accomplished by Jesus becoming a child in Bethlehem where He grew "in wisdom and statue and in favor with God and man." In other words, Jesus developed mentally, physically, spiritually, and socially and fulfilled His earthly mission. When the "God-part" of redemption was finished, Jesus on the Cross said, **"It is finished."** He had completed the work the Father had commissioned. In the command to His followers, the contract was passed down to those who remained on earth, when Christ returned to the right hand of power in heaven. Believers became sub-contractors working under Christ to complete the task of reaching the lost and meeting the needs of the disadvantaged. Christ gave His early followers a working commission that was passed on to us through the Scriptures and by spiritual leaders.

A Working Commission

The gospel tells us that following the resurrection, Jesus gave a working commission to the believers. The scriptural examples of early believers demonstrate that converts went everywhere proclaiming the good news about Christ and that God confirmed both the messengers and the message with wonderful and mighty works (Mark 16:19,20). The Holy Spirit is the present enabler and equipper of believers for the task at hand. The Spirit readily provides the resources, authority, and the opportunity for each believer to do God's work God's way and live a life larger than they otherwise could. There is a story of a gracious elderly lady who was mailing the old family Bible to her younger brother for safe keeping. The postal clerk asked, "Is there anything breakable in here?" The firm and clear answer was, **"Only the words of Jesus and the Ten Commandments."** We must never break the chain of evangelism that reaches back to the Cross of Calvary.

> *1.* ***As we work together with God,*** *we appeal to you not to accept the grace of God and let it go to waste. 2. (God said, I have heard your prayers at a convenient time, and in the day of salvation I have brought you relief in a difficult situation: observe, now is the time for coming together; now is the day of deliverance.) 3.* ***Habitually we give no occasion of stumbling that the ministry be discredited****: 4. On the contrary,* ***we seek to commend ourselves as God's ministers, by steadfast endurance****, in troubles, in hardships, in difficulties, 5. in flogging, in bonds, in angry mobs, in hard labor, in sleepless nights, in hunger; 6.* ***by innocence, by understanding, by long-suffering, by kindness, by the Holy Spirit, by authentic love, 7. by speaking the truth, by God's power, by weapons of righteousness, the sword of the Spirit in the right hand and the shield of faith in the left hand****, 8. by loss of civil rights yet remaining a citizen of the kingdom, by haters, but still loved by God: called a wandering quack, but* ***my message is true; 9. declared worthless without credentials by the Jews, but well known by the saints; always facing death, but truly alive; chastised, but not killed. 10. Sometimes grieved but always rejoicing; penniless, but enriching the souls of many; having nothing, and yet possessing everything****. (2 Corinthians 6:1-10 DNT)*

Encourage and Inspire Believers

The faith-based places of worship are there to encourage and inspire believers to carry the message to their daily contacts. This work takes place in homes, in the market place, and on the roadside, anywhere the lost will listen to the good news or any place of need in the community. These two go together. One cannot be sincerely interested in reaching the lost without a firm and clear witness that shows genuine concern for the lost, the hungry, the homeless, or the abused. Through the agency of the Spirit, there are people everywhere searching for the truth that born-again believers could supply. In the daily walk of believers there are doors of opportunity to pass through and be a faithful witness to those inside or those on the roadside. However, if they are hungry or homeless, they cannot listen. Scripture is clear, "The spiritual did not come first, but the natural: and afterward the spiritual," (1 Corinthians 15:46 DNT). At times the human needs must be met before the spiritual can be achieved.

Deacon, Take a Walk

A clear example that the primary work of believers is in the work-a-day world happened when one of the early deacons in Jerusalem listened to the Spirit and was told, **"Deacon, take a walk."** Philip obeyed and on his walk found a man seated in a chariot reading the scroll of Isaiah. Philip joined himself to the situation and asked, "Do you understand what you are reading?" The clear answer, "How can I unless someone explains this to me?" Was this man speaking of himself or someone else? **And at that time and place using the same scripture, Philip explained the good news to the man from Ethiopia.** When the stranger understood, he believed and requested baptism. When Philip made sure of his active faith, he was baptized, and he carried the Christian faith back to his homeland (Acts 8:26-39). Ethiopia is the oldest independent country in Africa, and the Christian church in Ethiopia owes its existence to the deacon's walk in the desert. All believers should clearly understand that the force that brought this Ethiopian into the kingdom remains at work; as believers walk the straight and narrow way they must take the gospel around the world. Obedience to the guidance of the Spirit is doing God's work God's way.

A Workable Plan

The facts about Philip and the Ethiopian clearly demonstrate a workable plan. God prepares the saint, creates the situation, puts the sinner in the right place, and provides available and useable materials for the presentation of the good news of Christ. This is God working with believers to serve individuals at their point of need. This is indeed God's plan: reaching individuals where they are and at their point of need at the earliest point in time, without requiring them to attend a place of worship. After one comes to a saving knowledge of Christ, they are then presented to the church for baptism and guidance in living the Christian life. In scripture no one was required to cross cultural or language lines to hear the gospel. The Spirit enables believers to establish a life-style and as they go about their daily business to witness to those being led by the Spirit and are ready to believe. Lifestyle, personal, hands-on sharing of the gospel is truly doing God's work God's way.

The Point of Greatest Need

To do God's work God's way one must meet individuals at their point of need and function as God's messenger of good will. Mankind works on easy solutions; God works at the point of greatest need. This must be understood if believers are to work together for the good of others. True togetherness is to be in agreement with God and having the best interest of others. It requires mutual acceptance of others and a willingness to jointly act on behalf of the greatest needs. This requires all believers to enlarge their life to reach the lost and needy and to work together with God and others to accomplish positive social change. It would be good to review Paul's admonition to the Corinthians. This caution and warning is relevant to the present needs of the church and all faith-based gatherings of believers. Paul's words show the range of endurance and cooperation when one is doing God's work God's way.

My Philosophy of Change

When asked about my philosophy of change and how I take advantage of an opportunity for constructive social or spiritual change? First, I understand the energy and effort placed into existing programs that may not be fully meeting the present needs of individuals and groups. The next step is to understand that one should not "Throw out the baby with the bath water!" All working elements of a corporate or organizational operation should be preserved with respect to those who have previously labored in the same vineyard or on the program or project. This is also true when working with individuals. One must look at and pay attention to the parents and family that brought the person to where they presently find themselves. Parents and families are not perfect, because they are human. However, there is no human problem or difficulty that divine intervention cannot improve. Social and spiritual change moves slowly, and all who would make a difference in groups or with individuals must be patient and understand the constant nature of change.

Change is Constant

Change is the one constant in life; however, all change is not positive. Change is the current flowing stream on which the circumstances of life are altered for the better with adequate guidance and sincere effort. To assure that changes in services, programs, and projects are positive, one needs a clear model for constructive change. Change in institutions, organizations, and groups is normally slower than change in most individuals. At times there is a divine interruption in one's life that produces drastic change. Normally, change is gradual and occurs over time, and to be positive change, guidance and direction by others is normally required. This constant effort toward positive change can create a seamless process that is smooth and healthy. Normally, the concept of W.A.S.P. would be followed using a simple acrostic for **C H A N G E**:

Consider the weakness of the present situation; (an honest assessment of both good and bad)

Have a viable plan of action; (develop a practical plan and move forward immediately)

Arrange priorities quickly; (determine existing resources and personnel and act)

Negotiate with others a way forward; (discuss areas of concern with others)

Gather a workable team, and (find effective people for a functioning team -- **TEAM** has no **"I"**)

Engage fully in constructive discussion to implement positive and productive change.

Continuous and Seamless Change

When considering positive change in an institution, organization, or community, all existing programs and personnel must be evaluated as to their adequacy for the present task. **If there are weaknesses or failures, one must correct the inferior before a superior can be constructed.** New efforts should blend into the work of others gradually and seamlessly so that it is impossible to see where one ends and another begins. We are in this process together. Individuals especially the young must not be separated from family and friends unless there is no other way to facilitate positive change. Programs and services of the community and the outreach ministry of the church should be evaluated and recommended changes phased into the process. Fix what needs to be fixed, fund what needs to be funded, replace what does not work, and move ahead together! The goal is positive spiritual and social change, one for all and all for one. At times, groups cannot be changed until a significant number, at least ten percent, of the group agree and are willing to be changed and to accept change for the group. This is the way group dynamics work and those who would produce positive change must understand this process. Otherwise, they could further slow the process of change. Every human plan has weaknesses and strengths. When both of these are understood and dealt with properly, the work can be completed and progress can be made toward positive change.

Weaknesses and Strengths Plan

In seeking positive change, one must assess the strengths and weaknesses of the present situation and always remain optimistic. **Negativity will not work, because a positive conclusion cannot be reached from a negative assumption.** Yet when one makes a positive declaration for social change it has an implied negative aspect about the present people, program, project, or policy. A "soft sale" is the answer. Although the present situation may have good parts, the existing entity is not completely adequate or the present needs would not exist. Statements for positive social change should be considered an acknowledgment of the prior achievements of others and that the present constructive moves are on the foundations of what was done in the past. In other words, we are working on a steady and continuous service to improve existing conditions, and the process should be seamless. Accomplishments of the past may have been good for yesterday, but may not be adequate for today. Yet they are the foundation stones upon which positive change must be built. Always consider that present changes may not be sufficient for tomorrow. Others will come along and improve on this work as they see the situation from a different perspective and may have new and fresh insights. It is a compliment when others improve existing programs.

Correcting the Inferior

Before positive change or a superior program can be put in place, the inferior aspects should be corrected or strengthened. Such efforts are usually under the banner of an effort known as **W**eaknesses **A**nd **S**trengths **P**lan (W.A.S.P.). In some circles the construct of W.A.S.P. is an offensive term meaning White Anglo-Saxon Protestant; in this case, it may be negative. Others may associate it with a wasp, a slender black-and-yellow-striped social stinging insect that one always attempts to avoid. Neither explanation is correct. In the case of positive social or spiritual change, one must see both the strengths and weaknesses of a person or a program as part of the path forward. Only when one is objective enough to see both sides can positive change result from the effort.

Weakness

And

Strengths

Plan

Team is a "We" Effort

The word and concept known as "team" to some suggests my side, my squad, our players, etc., as if they had ownership of the team members. TEAM always represents a group of individuals working toward a common goal. TEAM is always plural in nature. There is no place in teamwork for the personal pronouns such as, I, you, she, or he or substitutes such as myself, her, me, or myself. Teamwork is not a "me" thing; it is a "we" effort and is always the cooperative work by a group. This joint effort is collaboration and does not allow for personal credit. When two or more individuals work together to realize shared goals and the action is willing cooperation there are no heroes.

When Sir Edmund Hillary reached the top of Everest, he was not alone. He and a Sherpa mountaineer, Tenzing Norgay, became the first climbers (1953) known to have reached the summit of Mount Everest. When he returned to the base camp and met the press, the question was asked, "Who was the first man to stand on top of the world?" Hillary's answer was clear and concise, "We were on the same rope. We got there together."

It took courage to climb that mountain, but it was character and integrity that shared the credit for the climb. Surely, those who demonstrate remarkable acts and show great courage or strength should be recognized, but the honor goes to the TEAM. An acrostic of TEAM will clarify the work of such a group:

Treat the area of concern as a serious matter.

Endeavor to gather a group of compatible individuals.

Accumulate a working strategy and

Make an effort to gain consensus.

Why Join the Expedition?

TEAM suggests consensus and means agreement and harmony as to the assessment of weaknesses and strengths. Teamwork is constructive change with clear objectives that are fully articulated so individuals can factor into those objectives their personal goals. Leadership must always permit "group dynamics" to work to create a team spirit. People join a group because they believe their personal goals will be met when group objectives are achieved. Why did Tenzing join Hillary on the climb to the summit of Everest? It was his job as a guide, but he also wanted to reach the top of the world. Hillary's goals and Tenzing's goals worked together to get both to the summit on the "same rope." Mountain climbers assist each other. If one slips and falls, the other prevents a disaster. Solomon, the wise man, wrote, "Two are better than one...if they fall the other will lift up his fellow... but woe to him that is alone when he falls for he has not another to help him up," (Ecclesiastes 4:9, 10). If for a moment an individual thinks that personal goals will not be met, they will abandon the TEAM. Any loss of members or even silent resistance to positive change can cause failure in reaching positive objectives. Those leading the process of change must be fully aware of both the attitude and action of all within the group. Otherwise, there will be unavoidable conflict instead of positive change.

A Demonstrated Spiritual Effort

If the group is engaged in a spiritual effort, then the honor and glory goes to God alone. Of course, those who guide or direct the process of change should be recognized, but do not forget that nothing can be accomplished for God without the aid and guidance of the Holy Spirit. Individuals working alone or in groups must always understand the function of spiritual objectives that influence the outcomes of any effort. There is no "I" in TEAM, and all must subordinate personal wishes to the positive change agency of the Holy Spirit. God leaves room for other people to be a part of any spiritual effort. Team members should always remember that those who now work in any spiritual effort are standing on the shoulders of others. Spiritual change can come only through prayerful attention to the details of the situation and mutual concern for all involved in the process.

Protect Life and Limb

When considering the needs of a community, the living conditions of individuals are priority. The arrangements between parents and children are of paramount interest. The contacts and interaction between adults, community children, and the elderly must be evaluated. Any structure that does not protect the "life and limb" of children and the elderly must be dealt with drastically. There must be an orderliness of operation and practical arrangements for all members of the community. The efficiency and effectiveness of all services and programs must be assessed and weaknesses strengthened and the strengths utilized to benefit all concerned.

Sustainable Development of Families

An honest viewing of life from both ends of the spectrum is the only way to assure sustainable development of the family from birth to death. When parents neglect their children, the future of the family is in jeopardy. When children are abandoned by parents, the family is in effect dissolved. The results are then unacceptable because others must now assume the care of the children. Good and loving parents caring for their own children is always the best way; however, when children are neglected it is necessary for surrogate parents to care for their growth and development. When adults neglect the needs of children or elderly parents, the prolonged existence of family values are weakened or abandoned.

An Honorable Marriage

When parents fail to maintain a proper and honorable marriage in which to grow their family, God's two-parent plan is in jeopardy. Should believers, the community, or the organized church neglect either the children or the elderly they are subject to the wrath and judgment of God. Could such neglect be part of the growing crime in the community and the "no growth" in faith-based entities, the loss of appreciation for government entities, and the lack of relevance for places of worship? Should any of these occur there can be no sustainable development of the community and no room for the biblical model of the family. Such neglect without constructive change is planting poor seeds in poor soil. The harvest will then be poor and will produce even weaker seeds for the next generation. The rotten apples must be removed from the basket.

Bad Apples

If a rotten apple can spoil a whole basket of fruit, what can "bad apples" in the home and community produce? Just look around at the crime ridden communities filled with dysfunctional families and blinded observers who look the other way to avoid the tragic scenes. When the blind lead, all the people end up in the ditch of despair and depression with a hopeless future. A simple change in the spiritual aspects of the situation can produce good seed and assure a better community and family harvest in the future. Bad apples must be removed to limit their bad influence on the children and the community.

The Seed is in the Fruit

A principle established at Creation was "the seed is in the fruit," (Genesis 1:11). Each living thing reproduces itself with all the same essential components. Each element of God's Creation reproduced itself from the basic DNA (deoxy-ribonucleic acid), an essential component of all living matter, and the basic material in a cell that transmits the hereditary pattern. Bad parents, bad siblings, bad leaders, and the list goes on and on: each reproduce themselves. Even good seed in a bad environment will produce a weak plant that is normally short lived. Scripture is clear that "the fruit of a bitter root will corrupt many. The fact is that Esau, who sold his birthright for a bowl of soup, changed the future of succeeding generations (Hebrews 12:14-17).

Bad Seeds and Bitter Roots

It becomes clearer each day as one reads the daily newspaper or listens to the 24/7 news that families and communities are in trouble. Even the economies of Nations and the world are reaping the harvest of bad seeds from past and present generations. This trouble comes from "bad seeds" and from the "bitter roots" caused by neglect, abandonment, and abuse that are prevalent in society. The sad part is that it was preventable, and believers and faith-based groups are doing little if anything to restrain corruption that results in bad parents and incomplete and dysfunctional families. To rectify the situation, believers must be able to network and access the material and spiritual provisions provided by Providence. It takes planning, money, and energy to produce positive social and spiritual change in a community. The worse it gets the more energy and effort it takes to make a difference. The moral is to act immediately. Delay could be disastrous.

Involvement in Community Change

Responsible people and responsible government are answerable to both God and the electorate for all actions. This includes carrying out all required or constitutional duties including oversight and delegation of authority to agencies to make decisions independently. Then leaders must require conscientious and trustworthy behavior of all personnel together with the ability to provide an adequate budget to manage all known financial obligations. At times a responsible government will assist with worthy projects, but this does not release responsible people from pushing ahead to accomplish a worthwhile project.

Responsible People in Government will be:

Reliable and reasonable individuals accountable to the people;

Evenhanded in all dealings with individuals and the public;

Sensitive to and supportive of the needs of the electorate;

Predisposed to act for the welfare of the people;

Open-minded to all opportunities to advance social progress;

Neutral in religious and ethnic matters;

Steadfastness in times of national change or crisis;

Impartial in personnel and financial matters;

Budget allocations sufficient for administration and services;

Liable for all policies and errors in judgment or action;

Efficient in performance without loss or waste —

Steps to Positive Community Change

Regardless of who or how community projects to bring about positive change are initiated, the process is basically the same. When best practices are followed and accountable people act in a conscientious way, the outcome should be positive results. The normal steps are:

1. **Identify** community areas of concern: dysfunctional families, substandard housing, unresponsive government entities, presence of drugs and criminal elements, weak or limited schools, limited recreational opportunities, homelessness, limited employment, and the absence of functioning faith-based groups.

2. **Classify** priority projects and determine the resources required to produce positive change.

3. **Pinpoint** primary change needed within each area of concern.

4. **Transform** the specific needs into an action plan for each area of concern.

5. **Develop** an evaluation plan based on expected outcomes.

6. **Determine** the individuals, NGO's, private businesses, and governmental agencies that could provide assistance or guidance in specific areas.

7. **Gather** resources, people, and materials required and initiate action in the priority areas.

8. **Monitor** the process and progress and conduct outcome evaluations.

9. **Learn** from the process and utilize this knowledge in the next community.

10. **Provide** for on-going follow-up that demonstrates continued concern for local people and community leaders.

   8. And the master complemented his level-headedness: for the businessmen of the world are wiser in dealing with others than those with spiritual insight. 9. And I say to you, Make friends for yourselves by the wise use of money, so when the money is gone your friends will receive your eternal reward. 10. He who is faithful in small things is trustworthy in big things. 11. If you have not been faithful in the wealth of this world, who will trust you with true riches? 12. And if you have not been faithful with another man's wealth, who shall give you personal possessions? 13. No steward can serve two masters: he will hate one and love the other or attach himself to one and detest the other. You cannot serve both God and the false god of wealth. (Luke 16: 8-13 DNT)

Active Believers are Essential to Positive Change

Active believers are essential to positive change. Believers must learn how to access God's provisions; this is the key to an adequate service to both God and man. The government and the wealthy have a role in positive social change, but active believers connected to faith-based groups are essential to accessing God's provisions and guidance for positive ministry and social change.

   The Lord bless you and keep you; the Lord make His face shine upon you and be gracious to you; the Lord approve of you and give you peace, (Numbers 6:24-26 DOT).

AMEN!

CHAPTER SIX

PROVIDENTIAL PROVISIONS

But my God shall supply all your needs according to the
wealth of his glory by Christ Jesus. (Philippians 4:19 DNT).

Good News and Bad News

It is my conviction that God always supplies sufficient
funds to make faith-based organizations function adequately
to meet their spiritual mission. They may not have funds to do
the unnecessary things that bring enhancement to individuals,
but there will be funds for essential elements of God's program.
There may not be enough funds for elaborate facilities, but
there will be enough funds to maintain adequate places of
worship and sufficient outreach efforts to reach the lost.
There will also be enough funds to produce social and spiritual
change in the community. A story is circulating about a pastor
who announced one Sunday that he had good and bad news.

The good news was, **"we have enough money to build a
new church building."** The bad news was, **"it is still in your
pockets or your personal bank accounts."** God supplies
His people with funds for their family, to assist the poor, and
to share in the support of faith-based worship and outreach;
however, getting a reluctant giver to follow the plan of "tithes
and offerings" and supply funds needed to operate God's work
is a difficult task. This is the good news and the bad news:
God owns the cattle of a thousand hills and the gold in the hills,
but someone has to feed and milk the cows and others must
dig for the gold. God's blessings do not come to the idle.

Accessing Funds God Provides

It is understood from scripture that God takes care of spiritual work, and this includes funds to assist the needy. There
are various ways and means to fund God's work, but tithes and

free-will offerings seem to be God's master plan. Money does not grow on trees except for those who cultivate an orchard, but providential provisions are there for the asking when there is a genuine need. Perhaps a business where God is a partner can become a Financial Orchard where God provides provisions for the harvest. When a believer asks in faith to meet a genuine need, God will answer. The fruit must be harvested, but before the harvest comes there is a time of preparing the soil, planting the seed, cultivating the crop, caring for the growth, and making a timely harvest.

A delay in the harvest is normally due to human neglect. Fruit left on the vine too long is normally lost. Accessing God's provision has to do with positive action in a timely manner. The laborer is worthy of wages but not necessarily wealth. Yet God does not mussel the ox that treads out the corn. In other words, do God's work and God will provide the necessary funds to operate at the level of your faith and the quantity of the need. God does not provide for the laying up of treasures on earth. God's supply is not given to be stored for children who may or may not be a believer. Wealth is provided to support the present family and Kingdom work. Remember, the manna with which God fed Israel in the wilderness met a daily need. If more was gathered than was needed it spoiled. The warning is to use daily all that God provides for the work at hand. Work while it is day, and your endeavor will store treasures in heaven's storehouse. It has been said, **"Cast your bread on the water and God will return it with butter and jam."** Do not worry about tomorrow; each day takes care of itself in God's economy. God wanted his people to be the first matured and collected fruit by following what was right on the true course.

*16. **Do not wander from the right or deviate from the true course**, my cherished band of brothers. 17. **Every unspoiled and true benefaction is from above, and comes down from the Father of all light, with whom there is no changeableness, neither a dark side where there is no light.** 18. Of his own determination procreated as a Father all of us*

*with the expression of genuineness, that we should be the
first **matured and collected fruit** of God's created beings.
(James 1:16-18 DNT)*

The Windows of Blessings

It is firmly believed that God's work done God's way will
never lack God's supply. How does this work? When one
releases to God a small portion of what s in human hands,
what is in God's hands is released for God's work. The Prophet
Malachi was clear **that the way to open the windows of
blessings from heaven was to place a small portion of one's
resources into God's work** (Malachi 3:10-12). Although God
provides an abundant return on the small investment by believers, the return is for the family care and the corporate work of
the kingdom, not the enrichment of individuals. It was a scriptural challenge to validate God's promise of pouring out unlim-
ited blessings for His work when believers followed this plan.
The abundant blessing beyond the need was to be used for the
needs of others.

A Small Part

Tithing is one-tenth or a small part of income or produce
voluntarily provided in support of God's work. The tithe is not a
debt you owe, but a seed you sow! The harvest from the seeds
of tithe and offerings is the way God's work is supported when
it is done God's way. To deny God's storehouse the support of
tithe and offerings is to take from the hand of God the seeds
that would supply a bountiful harvest for Kingdom work. Surely
God has resources sufficient without our contributions, but
God chooses to use only those gifts that come from the people
to support Kingdom work. One should remember that tithing
alone is not sufficient to access the funds God provides. Living
a true and consistent Christian life is an important part of
accessing the funds God provides.

*10. Bring one-tenth of your income into the storehouse so
that there may be food in My House. Test me in this matter,*

*says the Lord who rules over all, and see if I do **not make the windows of heaven open and send down such a blessing on you until there is no room for it all.** (Malachi 3:10 DOT)*

*23. **You tithe** down to the last mint leaf in your garden, but ignore the important things – honest decisions, compassion, and moral conviction. Yes, you should tithe, **but you should not omit the more important things.** (Matthew 23:23 DNT)*

Tithing is NOT To Insure Promptness

To

Insure

Promptness.

The practice of the **T.I.P.** was initiated in merry old England in an effort To Insure Promptness. In the early English Pub there was a box at the door marked T.I.P. A customer in a hurry to return to work would drop a coin in the box, and the waiter hearing the coin drop would understand that the customer was in a rush. This would insure prompt service so the customer could return to work. It should be understood that **the tithe is not a TIP to rush God into action to make one prosperous**. Neither is tithing a debt one owes; it is part of God's plan to free workers from other tasks so they may concentrate on Kingdom work. True kingdom-minded believers are willing participants in the plan to underwrite those who make a full-time commitment to Christian service and support missionary efforts at home and abroad. Surely, tithing opens the windows of heaven, but that was not the reason for this God-given plan to support God's work.

Business has a Spiritual Purpose

Business is an organized effort to provide goods and/or services to others exchanged on the basis of perceived value. The early meaning of "business" related to being busy doing something practicable and profitable. Business requires an investment and a customer base. When a faith-based person enters business, it operates by moral standards in the context of a cultural and a spiritual environment. For a believer, God must be a partner in the enterprise, and moral ethics ought to permeate the whole endeavor. Not only must one follow the principles of responsible business, but a believer must consider the proper use of funds generated by the business. After the expenses including a fair wage for workers, what will be done with the net profit? Since God is a partner in the business, where will His share of the profit be placed? This should be determined after prayerful consultation as early as possible so the business plan will not stray from the spiritual purpose.

Delay in God's Business

During the rise in gas prices in some parts of the world, a pastor was waiting in line for lower priced gas. The attendant worked hard to service the cars on a holiday weekend. Finally, there was a vacant pump. The attendant said, "I'm sorry for the delay, but it seems people wait until the last moment to get ready for a long trip." With a smile, the pastor said, "I know what you mean. It's the same in my business." It is not good business to delay adequate preparation for the future whether it is business or eternity.

> 11. **Do not delay your enthusiasm; be on fire in the spirit; serving the Lord as a slave;** 12. *rejoice in hope; remain steadfast in time of trouble;* **be persistent in the habit of prayer; 13. contribute your share with reference to the needs of the saints; give attention to hospitality.** *(Romans 12:11-13 DNT)*

Take Care of God's Business

Business is an endeavor dealing with the public together with God's partnership with believers seeking to reach those in need. This means if you are in business...you are in business with God. Your behavior should demonstrate this knowledge.

Take care of God's business, and God will take care of your business. This story by Jesus speaks to this issue of doing business until the King returns. There are rewards for following instructions and making a profit for the King's business. Failure to "do business" as instructed also has consequences that are not pleasant. All believers should be determined to do God's work God's way.

Business is an organized effort to exchange values

Unleash an opportunity to sustain others

Swap and trade goods and services for resources

Industrious effort to make things better

Narrow the focus to profitable activities

Establishes a spiritual enterprise

Serious effort to generate needed funds

Support the area and cause of greatest need

*12. Jesus said, **A nobleman journeyed to a far place to obtain his kingdom and return**. 13. **He called ten servants and gave each about three month's wages, and said, Do business until I return**. 14. But his subjects continued to detest him and sent delegates, saying, We will not accept this man to reign over us. 15. When he came back as king, he commanded those servants to whom he gave funds, to account for the profit each had gained trading. 16. The first came, saying, Lord the profit has been ten times. 17. And he said, Well done, my good servant: because you have been faithful in this small thing, you will have authority over ten cities. 18. The second one came, saying, My profit has been five times. 19. And he said likewise to him, you will have authority over five cities. 20. And another came, saying, Lord, here is the money you gave me, I have kept it safe in a napkin: 21. For I was afraid, because you are a stern man: you pick up what you never put down, and harvest what you did not sow, 22. and he said, Out of your own mouth you have judged* *yourself, you worthless servant, you knew I was a stern man, picking up what I never put down and harvesting what I did not sow; 23.* **Why then did you not deposit my money into the bank that at my return I may receive back my money with interest? 24. And he said to those standing by, Take from him the money and give it to the servant who had the tenfold increase.** *(Luke 19:12-24 DNT)*

Wise use of Money

When the faithful have wealth, God requires a wise use of these funds. The practical use of wealth is regarded as an act of wisdom. Luke wrote, **"Make friends for yourselves by the wise use of money,"** (Luke 16:9 DNT). God blesses individuals with affluence and possessions and expects these material goods to be used for the good and advancement of Kingdom work. Doing God's business God's way produces capital assets that may become resources for God's work. Believers should not seek after wealth unless they have a clear plan to use it for the benefit of others. Greed and materialism have no place in God's work. Scripture is clear in the qualification for Christian service that those who serve in the Kingdom must not be "greedy after filthy lucre." It is alright to gain wealth provided it is earned in honesty and fairness. The idea of filthy lucre is money that is obtained by doing something bad. Although the "wealth of the wicked is stored up for the righteous," God guides those who would gain wealth to make friends and be faithful in even the small things.

Do Not Neglect or Withhold Funds

God charges high interest on delayed funds. In the Old Testament when one committed "a trespass against the holy things" even due to "ignorance," the Law required a twenty percent interest (add the fifth part thereto) be added to the principal (Leviticus 5:15, 16; 6:5) on any disobedience of God's commandments. The New Testament records, "Do not muzzle the ox that treads out the corn" (Deuteronomy 25:4).

17. Let the seniors **who practice oversight well be counted worthy of two-fold money, especially those who labor preaching and teaching.** 18. For scripture says, **You shall not muzzle the ox treading out the corn. And, the laborer is worthy of his compensation.**
(1 Timothy 5:17, 18 DNT)

Scripture records that those who preach the gospel should live of the gospel. When believers withhold or delay "tithes and offering" they will not prosper. Twenty percent is a high price for neglect or delay to fund religious workers. It is important to take care of the family, but this is not an excuse to deny the funds needed by faith-based workers. There are serious consequences to such action. It is much the same as buying a fuel-efficient auto without the power to get you to the church on time. This has become a fuel efficient age. At times the attempt to save funds does not produce positive results. A young man visiting a museum that had a display of fuel efficient vehicles was surprised to find an old horse drawn carriage. When he read the sign hanging on the back of the old carriage, he understood. The sign on the carriage was, **"Energy efficient vehicle -- runs on oats and grass. Beware of the exhaust."** Perhaps those who try to save funds that should be used to support faith-based groups will find the end results somewhat dissatisfying. The warning is clear "Do not withhold funds from kingdom work." There is no profit in such action.

13. You know that those who serve in the temple take their food from the temple. And those who attend regularly at the altar share in the sacrificial offerings. 14. ***In the same way the Lord has commanded that they who preach the gospel should live of the gospel.*** *(1 Corinthians 9:13, 14 DNT)*

Honesty is the Best Policy

My motto through the years has been, **"Promise less— deliver more."** Following the principles of business the funds gained are sanctified for the Master's use. In business and other dealings with people honesty is the best policy. This would be true even if there were no God and no hereafter. Sincerity, truthfulness, and basic integrity are the best principles of accessing the wealth of this world provided the purpose is to use funds acquired to advance God's work. God may not need our money, but it is wonderful that God permits believers to participate in building good will and advance the gospel. The objective is to wisely use wealth so that God's work can be done God's way.

> *10.* **He who is faithful in small things is trustworthy in big things.** *11. If you have not been faithful in the wealth of this world, who will trust you with true riches? 12. And if you have not been faithful with another man's wealth, who shall give you personal possessions? 13. No steward can serve two masters: he will hate one and love the other or attach himself to one and detest the other.* **You cannot serve both God and the false god of wealth.** *(Luke 10:10-13 DNT)*

A Relevant Business

What does it mean to be relational: to behave as family, to feel friendly, or behave as next of kin. If you are a believer then you become blood- relatives though the Cross of all other believers. All who would do honest business must keep their promises because "your word is your bond." Dependability is the proper word. It is a similar concept as the one used to describe a reliable and trustworthy man in scripture "And I will fasten him **as a nail in a sure place**," (Isaiah 22:23). This was leadership with fixed and permanent dependability. What does it mean to be a relevant business related to the community, appropriately structured, useable and applicable products, important even significant as a leader. A business is not a leader just because it was first; but because among others it stands out as a "brand."

Give what you Promise

5. This is why I thought **it necessary to send the brothers**

beforehand to complete the collection which you promised,
because I want the giving to be forthcoming and not out of
obligation. 6. Remember the saying, he who sows in a miserly
manner shall reap miserly; and he who sows generously
shall reap an abundant harvest. 7. Let every man give as he
purposed in his heart; not reluctantly or under constraint:
for God loves a prompt and willing giver. 8. Now God is
continually able to overflow you with self-sufficiency always
making you competent to pour out to the good of others: 9.
As it is written, his generosity is scattered to the poor; his love-
deeds are never forgotten. 10. Now he who supplies plenty
of seed for the planting also furnishes bread for your table,
and multiplies the seed sown and increases the fruit of
your benevolence; 11. Your being enriched unto all liberality
causes us to give thanks to God. 12. The rendering of this
benevolence not only supplies the needs of the saints, but
causes a wealth of thanksgiving to God; 13. By evidence of
this service they glorify God for your conviction and response
to the gospel of Christ and for your liberality in sharing with
others; 14. And by their intercession for you their earnest
desire goes out to you to surpass your grace and generosity.
15. Thanks to God for his indescribable generosity to you. (2
Corinthians 9:5-15 DNT)

Giving Beyond their Means

Paul was both appreciative and concerned about the
generosity of particular groups of people who gave funds for
the poor. He commended them and classified their effort as
a good example to others. Tithing and giving multiplies the
resources and enables the church to care for the needy.

Generosity and Poverty

1. Moreover, brethren, we call your attention to the churches
of Macedonia who have already received a deposit of the
grace of God; 2. How their heavy affliction has proved their
joy and steadfastness and out of their deepest poverty has
come the richness of their generosity. 3. Spontaneously and
voluntarily, I bare record and affirm, that beyond their means

*without request and without coercion **they willingly gave of themselves**; 4. Urging us with much petition to receive **their gifts for the poor**, and take upon us **the sharing of the relief work** for the holy ones in Jerusalem. 5. And this they did, not as we expected, but they by God's will **have altogether given their own selves** to the Lord and to us. 6. This caused us to urge Titus to complete the task he had begun, that you might also **have the same grace of giving**. 7. Since you abound in almost everything, in faith and teaching, in knowledge of the truth and thoroughness, and **in your benevolent love, see that you also abound in the grace of giving**.* (2 Corinthians 8: 1-7 DNT)

Honest Administration of Funds

Paul understood how easy it was to criticize fundraising efforts. He went to great pains to place qualified and honorable people in charge of funds. This set a good example for others that all individuals associated with faith-based funds must have the respect and trust of the people.

Avoid all Suspicion

*18. And we have sent with him a beloved brother whose praise is in the good news throughout all the churches; 19. And not only that, but he was selected by the churches to travel with us with this generous gift, which is administered by us to honor the Lord and show our willingness to help: 20. **Avoiding all suspicion or blame, we took precaution in the administering of this large fund: 21. providing for honest arrangements both in the sight of the Lord, and also in the eyes of men**. 22. Along with them I am sending another brother, whose devotion we have often tested in many ways, but now more conscientious because of the great confidence I have in you. 23. As for Titus, he is my partner and fellow worker concerning you: as for our brethren they are messengers of the churches, and an honor to Christ. 24. Wherefore **demonstrate your benevolent love to them** before the churches, and justify my pride in you.* (2 Corinthians 8: 18-24 DNT)

Sharing the Burdens of Others

2. Practice in sharing the heavy burdens of others, and you will fulfill the principles of Christ. 3. If a man supposes himself to be something when he is really nothing, he deceives himself. 4. Let every man test himself for innocence, and then he shall rejoice in himself and not in another. 5. For **every man must carry his own personal load**. *6.* **Let him who receives instructions in the word share in support of the teacher's living.** *7. Be not deceived; no man can snub God:* **for whatever a man may sow this also he will reap**; *8. For he who plants proceeds in the field of the flesh shall have a spoiled harvest; but he who plants proceeds in the field of the Spirit shall harvest life everlasting. 9.* **And let us not become weary in doing what is right: for if we do not weaken our resolve, in due season we will collect the good harvest. 10. As we have opportunity, let us practice generosity to all, especially to those who are of the household of faith.** *(Galatians 6:2-10 DNT)*

Attitude Determines Advantages

It appears that the attitude and action of believers is tested in their predisposition to respond to the needs of others. The grace given to believers should be sufficient to allow a prayerful attitude toward even their enemies. In fact, scripture charges believers to love and pray for your enemies and even lend money to them expecting nothing in return. This appears to be a test God uses to measure obedience and sacrifice for the cause of Christ. When a believer clearly demonstrates a positive attitude toward those who are strangers, opponents, even adversaries, the love of God and the light of the gospel shines brightly upon them. Loving and showing kindness to even enemies is part of the witness to the saving grace of Christ. Scripture is clear, "A soft answer turns away wrath." Also, the phrase before the "Golden Rule" is often overlooked because it appears to not be logical. **"Give to everyone who asks: and ask not for the return of goods taken. And as**

you wish that men may do to you, do you to them likewise," (Luke 6:30, 31 DNT).

The Essence of Charity

The concept of "ask" here is "asking because of personal need." This is the essence of Christian charity: kindness, compassion, and generosity. The Christian ethic is positive. It does not suggest refraining or "not doing" but clearly points to "actively doing" good things. In ancient China, Confucius was asked if the language contained one word that would serve as a rule for all of life. His answer was a word that comes through French diplomacy into English meaning "reciprocity." I am certain that Confucius was not thinking of dealings between states; the question had to do with "a word that contained a rule for all of life." It is a mutual exchange between two parties to the advantage of both and even suggests putting yourself in another man's shoes. There is an old Indian saying, "Never judge another man until you have walked a mile in his shoes."

A Better Way

The law of retaliation (Exodus 21) gave many regulations concerning injury and damage, but Jesus showed a better way when He informed believers of a positive response when a Roman soldier compelled him to carry his load for a mile, "And whoever compels you to go a mile, go with him two," (Matthew 5:41 DNT). Love your enemies, turn the other cheek, and go the second mile may seem many steps too far to carry another's load, but it is the Christian way. The comprehensive scripture below speaks directly to this issue and declares that God expects the attitude and behavior of believers to be much different than those who do not follow Christ. Read it carefully. In addition to tithe and offerings, it is part of the way to access providential provisions. It may not seem to be man's way, but it is God's way.

Do Not Expect a Return

27. But to all who hear me I say, **Love your enemies, do good to those who hate you.** *28. Praise them that attempt to harm you,* **and pray for them who attempt to damage you out of small-mindedness.** *29. And to him who strikes you with violence on one cheek offer the other also; and to him who takes your outer garment, give him also your undergarment. 30.* **Give to everyone who asks: and ask not for the return of goods taken. 31. And as you wish that men may do to you, do you to them likewise.** *32. For when you love those who love you, what kind of thanks is freely given? For those who habitually do wrong also love those who love them. 33. And if you are good to those who are good to you: what kind of thanks is freely given? For sinners also do the same. 34. And* **if you lend to those of whom you expect to receive, what thanks have you? For sinners also lend to sinners, to receive as much again. 35. But love your enemies and lend without expecting a return; and your reward shall be great; and you shall be the children of the Highest:** *for he is kind to the unthankful and to the evil. 36. Be compassionate, as your Father is also merciful and forgiving. 37. Do not pass judgment, release others from blame, and you shall not be condemned. 38.* **Give and others will press gifts into the pockets of your garment and good measure will be yours. For the same standard you use in giving shall be used to measure gifts to you.** *(Luke 6:27-38 DNT)*

God's Special Frequency

One may best access the funds God provides by listening to God's voice and obeying the clear message. If you did not understand or accept the words of the preceding scripture about the proper attitude and action toward enemies, perhaps you should remove anything that keeps you from tuning in to the holy ground frequency. When God spoke to Moses from the burning bush in the desert, the sound came from a special frequency. It appears that sound comes through electromagnetic waves and frequencies called **RF** (radio frequency), and to receive the sound one must be tuned into the proper frequency. In the case at hand, **RF** could stand for **R**edeeming **F**aith which is brought to mankind on waves of grace and can be used to see the positive potential in others. Moses heard the voice of God and understood his task of delivering God's people from bondage in Egypt. When Moses heard and understood the message, he was standing on Holy Ground and was instructed to take off his shoes to make better contact with God's holy frequency. Getting in touch with the holy ground and God's special frequency is necessary to "hear and behave" the word of God (Exodus 3:5).

Needs not Wants

In spite of the gold, glory, glamour, and the artificial prosperity some teach, God does not promise to fulfill all of the "wants" in the lives of believers; God promises to supply all the needs (Philippians 4:19 DNT). How are these needs met? How does one access the funds God provides? Simply ask in faith, and in God's timing it will come when it is needed to complete the mission or task God has given to you.

God does not Fund the Slothful

God does not fund the lethargic or the slothful; it is the active and vigorous who receive God's supply for kingdom work. Releasing the energy and the resources in your hand will open the hand of God to supply the needs for your ministry. The Genesis principle "earn your bread by the sweat of your brow" remains in effect. God rewards those who labor in His vineyard and causes the vineyard to grow and flourish. God promises to supply "needs" not "wants" to those who participate in His plan.

Paul reminded the Philippians of God's supply, *"But my God shall supply all your needs according to the wealth of his glory by Christ Jesus,"* (Philippians 4:19 DNT).

More than the Tithe is Needed

God blesses believers to be a blessing *to* others.
Believers should tithe both time and talent. To sacrificially
work as a volunteer is to turn energy into a valuable material
asset. It takes time and energy to earn money; however, giving
a tithe is not sufficient. The tithe is for corporate work. Special
projects and programs need additional gifts and offerings. The
generous giving appears to multiply individual blessings. Not
only in personal material benefits, but there are both personal
and spiritual blessings that come with the knowledge that
one has assisted the mission of the church and brought relief
to the poor and needy. One must also give time, talent, and
energy directly to a worthy cause. In fact, at times it is more
important to provide "hands on" assistance than to provide just
money. Although money represents one's time and energy, it is
vital that one become personally involved in assisting others.
Money is so abstract; people need to see both the kind face
and caring hands of the person behind the giving. Believers
should remember that doing what is right will bring God's
blessings.

> 9. *And Jesus said,* **Ask, and it will be given you; seek, and
> you will find; knock, and it will be opened to you.** *10. For
> every asker receives, and every seeker finds; and* **to him who
> knocks the door will be opened.** *(Luke 11:9, 10 DNT)*

Energy and Money

Energy can be exchanged for money. With money one can
hire the energy of others. To fully understand the support of
faith-based groups, one must realize that both labor and funds
are needed. Those who have money may donate the funds to
purchase material and hire labor. Some who wish to assist a
particular cause but do not have available funds may volunteer
their services to assist a faith-based group. It should be obvious that one cannot buy themselves out of responsible labor.
There are times that even money is not enough, when what a

faith-based group needs is "hands and feet" on the property. Workers, teachers, ministers, counselors, medical people, childcare workers, cooks, janitorial services, and many other areas of need can be supplied by the energy of volunteers. The labor of a volunteer is worth more than money; it is a personal "hands on" demonstration of genuine interest in the cause. When one is willing to get their hands dirty or put their back into the work, their example is of great value to the cause. When available funds are used to hire work or service that could be supplied by volunteers, the cause has been weakened, and the strength of the operation has been damaged or hindered. When a real need is presented to believers, a generous response of both funds and energy is normally forth coming. This has been the case during the history of God's dealing with the human race.

> 5. And as soon as the commandment came abroad, the children of Israel **brought in abundance** the first fruits of corn, wine, and oil, and honey, and of all the increase of the fields; **and the tithe of all things brought they in abundantly.**
> (2 Chronicles 31:5 KJV)

Networking Assures Progress

A wealth of wisdom can be found in a dedicated group of individuals with a common purpose. Networking is one of the tools that can gather this wisdom and advance a common cause. Formalizing and maintaining friendly relationships with people is important to any cause. This is even more important when such friendship could bring advantages and opportunities to a project. When people work together as a unit and systematically discuss and plan for progress in a given area, great things happen. A cooperative network of people with a common cause can produce much more than a single effort. When a group of people truly enjoy working together to reach agreed upon goals, there is a synergy or extra effectiveness that occurs that is powerful. A group working together produces greater accomplishments because of the addition of individual capabilities. Networking combines extra energy and effort to assure greater achievements. A network is a group working to build and maintain friendly relationships that bring advantages to a cause or project. More information is combined in the acrostic below:

Networking opens communications among colleagues

Establishes informal relationships for common action

Treats everyone as equals in a united cause

Watches over a well-organized plan to assure progress

Organizes people and resources for achievement

Regularly interacts to gain improved consensus

Keeps pushing forward toward agreed objectives

Introduces fresh ideas and information to others

Nurtures cooperative action for reaching goals

Groundwork for sustainable development

The Believer's Network

Normally the average believer does not have sufficient finances to fund God's work alone. This is why believers network to place their tithes and offerings into a central storehouse so it can be distributed according to need. In this day the church is not alone, there are many faith-based groups, Christian businessmen, NGO's, and government agencies that provide funds for worthy causes. Believers must be bold in seeking for these funds to be applied and properly used for the poor and needy. The Kingdom does not need more and larger buildings in which to sing and praise God; the world needs more large-hearted believers who will go into the world and serve the needs of others and thereby demonstrate the spirit and love of Christ to the lost. This is the way to do God's work God's way.

A Purpose of Heart

When an individual has purpose of heart, they are moving in a single direction toward a reachable goal. When a purpose is established it means that a decision has been made as to what is important and what ought to be accomplished. According to Scripture one may establish purpose by good counsel and good advice (Proverbs 20:18). Barnabas counseled the converts at Antioch "that with purpose of heart they should cleave unto the Lord," (Acts 11:23). He wanted the new believers to have a readiness and an eagerness to serve the Lord that included a promptness of action in all spiritual matters. This is the mind-set that promptly and sincerely acts when there is a need. In reality it is doing God's work God's way.

Now unto him who is able to do over and above all we ask or think, according to the power at work in us, may he be glorified in the church through Christ Jesus for all generations world without end. Amen! (Ephesians 3:20, 21 DNT).

Are you willing to be on God's work crew?

CHAPTER SEVEN

PEOPLE, PROPERTY, & POVERTY

Kicking the Downtrodden

It seems that most people want a front seat at the theater, a back seat at church, and the center of attention wherever they are. These selfish and uncaring attitudes usually cause such people to overlook or look down on the oppressed and down-trodden. This is **called kicking someone when they are down.** This is done in different ways. Some are overt when people are intentionally avoided because of their poverty or disadvantaged position. Then at times there are indirect or unknown discriminations when people look at those who are experiencing misfortune and feel that the poor or the troubled bring the conditions on themselves. Some people think the individual has done something bad to cause the poverty or living conditions in which they find themselves. This is often done without any sense of the antecedent causes of the plight of the poor. Most poverty results from the action of others. At times it is generational; at other times it is the result of family dysfunction. When it comes to the children, God sees them as innocent victims of the sins of others. Believers are instructed to give careful consideration to women alone and needy children.

Innocent Victims

Many who find themselves in the poverty category are victims of discrimination, hiring practices, government policies, a less than adequate school system, and perhaps most tragic of all is the presence of drugs and a criminal element that imposes restrictions and limitations on a particular community. It becomes clear that poverty is often caused by the action of others. Victims find themselves disadvantaged with no way to change their circumstance because a parent, who cannot work, cannot find employment or is able to work, but will not seek it. Then there is the neglect of basic parenting required to care for the little ones that determines the social and financial condition of the children. And at times it is an older sibling or relative who brings drugs or other criminal activities into the home, and the children suffer. Parents who do not adequately control the home environment and permit harmful activities are to blame for some of the existing poverty. Wasteful adults who do not manage their money often join with criminal activity as a quick money fix. Others who avoid criminal activity just accept their state of affairs because they have no hope of things getting better. These elements produce the major causes of poverty. Then there are the slum landlords who take advantage of the less fortunate and do not provide affordable and/or livable housing. Perhaps God has reserved a special eternal place for slumlords that neglect property and overcharge tenants.

Invest in God's Work

The poor hear the gospel with gladness; therefore, the message of peace and grace must be taken to the deprived areas and the underprivileged. They have needs, and their eyes and hands are open. Meeting their needs can also open their hearts to the gospel of Christ. There is an saying, **"Spend and be spent for the gospel."** This simply means that available resources are to be invested though the generosity of willing hearts and the ready energy of believers. This is spending and being spent, to take the gospel message to the poor and the disadvantaged. By advancing the cause of the poor who are open to the gospel, the investment of time, energy, and funds in people, property, and poverty will bring returns in both souls and satisfaction that comes with a job well done. It is clear that believers ought to regularly invest in the work of God as "seed money" that will bring a great harvest. Some fields are uncultivated and unproductive, yet others are ripe for the harvest, and believers should pray to the Lord of the harvest to send more willing workers. Are you willing to be on God's work crew?

God Multiplies the Seed Sown

*9. As it is written, **his generosity is scattered to the poor;** his love-deeds are never forgotten. 10. **Now he who supplies plenty of seed for the planting also furnishes bread for your table, and multiplies the seed sown and increases the fruit of your benevolence;*** (2 Corinthians 9:9, 10 DNT)

Practice Generosity to all

*9. And let us not become weary in doing what is right: for if we do not weaken our resolve, **in due season we will collect the good harvest.** 10. As we have opportunity, let us practice generosity to all. (Galatians 6:9 -10 a DNT)*

The Needs of the Poor

Some choose to criticize or belittle the downtrodden poor and the disadvantaged not realizing but for the grace of God they could be in the same mess. A failure to show true compassion toward those in need is to blatantly ignore the Golden Rule that clearly challenges the bystander with these words, **"Do unto others what you would have them do unto you."** This rule in various forms can be found in most writings of the major religions of the world. Can you imagine yourself tired and weary without a place to sleep, hungry, cold, and friendless? What would you have others to do for you if you were in such a tight spot? Would you still believe that it is more blessed to give than to receive? To have shelter, clothes, and food is a basic necessity, yet many poor endure daily without the basic necessities of life. They exist because the will to live is perhaps the strongest drive of the human race. The big question: what can or will you do about the needs of the poor? Some say, "The poor we have with us a ways." The big question is, "Why?"

Divine Nurturing Attributes

What is the quality of your spiritual DNA: that is your Divine Nurturing Attributes? God places within the heart and soul of each person the ability to care, encourage, and qualities for regarding the needs of others and acting responsibly. Even wild animals will feed and care for the offspring of animals outside their species. Can believers not muster the same maternal instinct and demonstrate paternal concern for the cold, hungry, and those without shelter? You may assess your own Divine Nurturing Attributes by determining your interest and willing involvement in the welfare of others. Do you encourage and foster the development of the young? Are you involved in providing tender, loving care and protection to the needy? Do you feel disposed to assist the poor and needy? Is your spiritual DNA worth reproducing? Will others see your good works and glorify God? Would you want to pass on your attitude and action to others? It has been suggested that each person called of God should endeavor to reproduce at least ten others with the same disposition and attitude to assist others. What could you change to improve your Divine Nurturing Attributes? Could you become a better mentor, advisor, counselor, guide, teacher, parent, mate, or soul-winner?

A Worthy Investment

God expects all believers to have a kindness in their heart for others, especially those in need. This kind compassion will prompt believers with purpose of heart to serve the needs of others. When a need is observed, without delay, true believers will act to timely meet the disadvantaged at their point of need. This normally prompts an investment of time and energy. Any investment in people, property, and poverty is a worthy enterprise, and the increase in value is worthy of both the time and effort. There is an excellent return on such an investment when God blesses the effort. One cannot really show concern for people without observing property and poverty. The quality of the infrastructure, the nature of public buildings, the neighborhood homes, and the general health and welfare of the people are all tied together. When one aspect of the group of three (people-property-poverty) is improved, the other two seem to follow close behind. When people have better living quarters they tend to take better care of themselves and their families. When the people themselves gain a better self-image and move toward self-improvement, usually their property shows change. Some of the causes of poverty are dysfunctional families, greedy landlords who are blind to the needs of the people, police who permit drugs and crime to exist in the community, and individual believers and local churches who are "blind, deaf, and dumb" when it comes to the needs of others. They are blind because they do not open their eyes and dumb because they do not speak out against absentee fathers, substandard housing, under nourished children, abused women, and abandoned and abused children. Yet, a little effort to improve people, property, and poverty goes a long way in changing the future for families and communities.

Use What You Have

The story of David and Goliath speaks to the issue here. Poverty and evil are enemies of God's people, and someone must go against them. David could not wear Saul's armor because he had not practiced to function with such weight. David was a shepherd boy with only the clothes he normally wore to care for sheep. He had no sword or shield. There were no bodyguards or armor bearers. David was alone with his love for God and the strength and talents he had used to kill the lion and bear that harassed the flock. He had confidence in himself and in his God that he could prevail against the enemy. With five smooth stones in his shepherd's bag and a sling he faced the giant in the name of Lord. With one fling of the sling a stone hit the giant in the head, and he fell dead. David cut off his head and took his armor. David was victorious, not by using the sophisticated armor of the King, but by using his spiritual aptitude and what he had. Each believer has sufficient strength, available weapons, and the protective covering of the Spirit to conquer the enemies of abuse, neglect, crime, and poverty (1 Samuel 17).

A Willing Blindness

Satan offers many things to distract believers from their appointed rounds to assist the needy. They become side-tracked with less important matters. Their attention is diverted to other things with little spiritual benefit. Some desire to be amused and entertained instead of investing time and energy in assisting the poor or witnessing to the lost. There seems to be a fallacy of forever getting ready. They go to church, attend evangelism classes, make pledges to foreign missions, teach Sunday school, work in church related sports with young people, even volunteer their time to sing in the choir or visit the sick and shut-in, but never do they get around to working on behalf of the poor and needy of the community. Their eyes are blinded from seeing the difficulties that honest and decent poor folk suffer, especially the children. This is not to account for the crime and meanness that the poor must endure in their neglected communities. Some spiritual eye salve is needed to remove the scales and clear up the vision of those who do not see the needs around them. This spiritual blindness creates a self-centeredness that creates a selfish attitude toward the needy of the community. What will a person give in exchange for the essence of a productive spiritual life?

Primary Concern is People

The primary concern is for the people living in the community. One cannot only see the population as a whole. It is the individuals who are the ones in need of assistance. An over-all view of a community can establish benchmarks by which individuals can be measured. When one observes the average assets and benefits enjoyed by a majority of the community, often the individuals who fall through the cracks of society are overlooked. When the normal standard of living is not enjoyed by all the community, some are deprived of human dignity that includes the loss of self-respect, employment problems, and often hunger and homelessness. It is not just the people; it is the persons individually: the neglected or abused child, the battered spouse, the sick, the physically challenged, the victims of crime, the criminal element, and the individuals who are responsible but are deficient in their duties. All of these must be observed and evaluated.

The Condition of Property

A close observation of property in a community can become a precursor to understanding the needs of the people. Abandoned, dilapidated, or rundown buildings usually mean that people are also neglected. When public buildings are in disrepair and public roads are not maintained, this could mean that community leaders have neglected their responsibility or are just derelict in their duties. It could be that they are poor managers of resources or are unable to set their priorities, but most likely they have little concern for the people who put them in office. Observing abandoned buildings covered with graffiti suggests the presence of a criminal element. Seeing substandard housing and the poor existing in shacks may mean that community and faith-based leadership are unaware of the causes and therefore the cure for such poverty. Material possessions, homes, cars, and discretionary funds are indicators of the division between the haves and the have-nots. When it takes all of the family income to just exist or when the breadwinner is unemployed or under employed, the scarcity and shortage will become obvious to anyone who cares.

The Rise from Poverty

A desire to eliminate poverty is a signal that one cares for the people. In reality an investment in poverty is a deposit in Heaven's Treasure Chest, and the increase in value is far beyond riches. Poverty suggests scarcity, deficiency, shortage, and hardship. The knowledge that one has assisted individuals to rise above an existence in abject poverty is a reward that cannot be purchased with money. It is also clear that a boot-strap operation does not work because it requires the poor to lift themselves out of a hopeless and miserable situation by their own efforts. Relying solely on the poor's own efforts and resources is not sufficient to change the level of poverty. This cannot be done without outside assistance. At times most individuals need hands on assistance or "a hand up" to get on their feet. Although such assistance will include material things, it must be more than material necessities; moral and spiritual values must be demonstrated and presented by a caring human face in the process. The rise from poverty really begins in the heart and soul of an individual with an increase in self-respect and a hopeful view of the future. The first step is to provide one with a positive outlook on life that breeds hope for tomorrow and the day after. The poor or neglected must never see personal assistance as a "one time" event. Whether the assistance is food, shelter, clothing, or a means to earn money, they must be able to see beyond today and tomorrow. With a hopeful view of the future, the journey out of poverty has begun. The following acrostic describes the essence of poverty.

Presence of hardship and scarcity

Obscurity and darkened hopes

Violation of human dignity

Existence of crime and violence

Reduction of living standards

Tired and troubled inhabitants

Yearning for a better way of life.

An Investment in Poverty

Poverty is a scarcity of essential things, a shortage of food, clothing, and shelter combined with crime, hardship, and human misery. A concern for the poor and needy begins with an observation of the existing living conditions of the family and/or individuals. A venture into the arena of the deprived and disadvantaged poor means investment in both people and property. When one becomes concerned for the needy they will become aware of their lack of material assets. With little funds for food and clothing, where will they find money for adequate shelter?

The Long-term Neglect of the Poor

Christian conversion often opens an understanding that the long-term neglect of the poor has enriched many. Such social guilt is revealed in the conversion of Zaccheus when he said, **"Lord, the half of my goods I will give to the poor and if I have taken anything wrongly, I will restore four times the amount."** And Jesus said, "This day has salvation come to this house," (Luke 19:8 DNT). Another example is presented in the decision of the Young Rich Ruler. **"Yet one thing you lack: sell all your possessions, and distribute it among the poor, and you will have treasure in heaven,"** (Luke 18:22 DNT). The rest of the story is that this particular individual decided not to follow the plan, and he went away in sorrow. The unwritten and unspoken words are obvious, **"And Jesus let him go."** No one is forced to follow the clear instructions recorded to assist the poor, but doing God's work God's way brings great blessings for obedience.

Learning the Lesson

This does not mean that all resources presented to assist the poor or all gifts provided to advance the ministry of believers is the result of social guilt. Often it is simply the result of a change of heart or the redemption of the soul that opens the eyes of believers to the needs and opportunities to assist kingdom work. There is a true blessing in giving to assist others. When this is clearly seen, God's work does not suffer from a lack of funds. Learning the lesson of planting good seeds in good ground and seeing a good harvest is a great benefit to the cause of Christ in the world.

One can Never do More Than is Needed

Normally the word "success" is not used in ministry or in dealing with social issues such as poverty because it suggests more than enough. It is clear that one can never do more than is needed. In fact the scripture is clear that when believers do all that was commanded they remain unprofitable servants because one can never do more than is enough for a good cause. When one does only part of what is needed and stops before producing a desirable result, the effort was unproductive and unprofitable.

*10. So likewise when you have **done all those things commanded** of you, say, We are **unprofitable servants**: we have done that which was our duty. (Luke 17:10 DNT)*

To use the word "success" in relation to ministry and service to others, particularly in the arena of social issues, is to suggest that one has done more than enough. This can never be the case. Sufficient to each day is the growing need for action on behalf of the poor and needy. Evil grows and poverty spreads like a disease. We must never be satisfied with what was accomplished yesterday when we see clearly the growing needs of today. Tomorrow will bring even more opportunities for social and spiritual challenge and change.   When we have done all that we can do there is still no claim to success because we have just done our duty.

*As we have opportunity, **let us practice generosity to all**, especially to those who are of the household of faith (Galatians 6:10 DNT).*

In addition to worship and Christian education believers must take advantage of each and every opportunity to share the good news and to serve the needs of others. No one will listen to your testimony of faith if they are hungry. No one will attend worship service or church actives if they do not have proper clothing. Those who are sick do not need a sermon. The homeless or the abused and neglected do not need worship and praise; they need the personal attention of an individual who cares and can demonstrate the love of Christ.

A Functioning Congregation

James wrote to scattered believers without available spiritual shelter. It may have been as long as one hundred years before believers began to build church buildings. James writing as an Elder in the church at Jerusalem presents the ethical aspects of Christian life. He clearly points out that there is a difference in knowing in the mind the truth that should be lived daily and the practical living out the Christian life daily. James gave them guidance in prayer, singing, dealing with the sick and needy, how to repair broken relationships, how to utilize the power of personal prayer, and how to return those who stray to the right path and make them useful to the congregation. Few specific guidelines for worship are given; obviously, James saw all of Christian action as "worship" or a positive response to God. Notice the sequence and the priority order of activities. Look closely at James 5:13-20 below:

Worship and Leader's Responsibility

*13. Is any among you **troubled**? Let him **pray**. Is any in **good spirits**? Let him **sing hymns**. 14. Is any **sick** among you? Let him **personally call for the senior leaders of the congregation**; and **let them earnestly perform their vows and pray with him, anointing with oil in the name of the Lord:** 15. Prayer offered in faith will restore the sick, and the Lord will furnish relief; provided there were transgressions; the brother (believer) will be exempted from further penalty.*

Repair Broken Relations

16. Acknowledge your failures and side steps one to another, and pray one for another, that you may be made whole again.

Utilize Personal Prayer

When a righteous man prays fervently there is great power in his prayer. 17. Elijah was a man similar to us and he prayed earnestly that it should not rain, and for three years and six months no rain fell upon the earth. 18. And he prayed again and the heaven gave rain; and the earth put forth her fruit.

Return Strays to the Right Path

*19. My band of believers, if any of you **do stray from the true path**, and one turn him about; 20. Let the brother know, **that he who turns a brother back from the error of his way into the right path** covers many faults and makes him safe, restoring his **usefulness to the congregation.** (James 5: 13-20 DNT)*

Spectators not Participants

A major difficulty in the worship services of today is that there are often more spectators than participants. These same spectators go out into the community and simply see the need and do nothing. These silent soldiers who do not obey the commands of the Holy Spirit will soon lose face and perhaps even faith in their ability to assist the less fortunate. Why? It is because they are preoccupied with their own needs and cannot see the urgency of the needed action they should take to assist the less fortunate. Such individuals will usually become a quick casualty of the spiritual battles waged by the evil forces in the world.

Some Shoot the Wounded

Without clear understanding of personal spiritual needs of those who neglect the needy and fail even to witness to their faith, the church often culls such individuals from the roll and have no further contact with them. In effect this is as if an army would shoot the wounded rather than care for the casualties of battle. What this suggests is that those who fail to witness and learn the lessons of faith and neglect to actively seek to lessen the suffering of others will soon become a victim of their own neglect. This is a tragic loss of energy that could be used for the kingdom, to say nothing of those who turn back from the right path.

To Neglect the Needy is Scandalous

When the poor are neglected, it is normally the little children who do most of the suffering. Scripture is clear that to neglect children is to offend them, and God's punishment is harsh for such disregard. Jesus said, **"Whoever receives little children in my Name, receives me."** The opposite would be true: those who reject children actually are rejecting both Jesus and God the Father, and the consequences are disastrous. In fact, it is scandalous. The Greek word for "offend" actually means "to cause to stumble, entrap, trip up, or entice to sin." The English word for "offend" is to scandalize. To neglect children or the elderly is disgraceful, immoral, shameful, and shocking. True believers will not forsake the needy or become involved in scandalous behavior. Jesus saw the neglect of children a serious matter. Consequently, caring for the needy is a necessary step in spiritual progress. Notice below the true consequence of causing a child to stumble or enticing them to sin. Jesus loved children. Do you want to be like Him?

> *36. And he took a little child, and placed him among them: and when he had taken him in his arms, he said, 37. Whoever receives (for themselves) little children in my name, receives me: and whoever shall receive me, receives not me alone, but him that sent me ....41. For whoever gives you a cup of water to drink in my name, because you belong to Christ, I assure you, he will not lose his wages. 42. **And whoever shall cause to stumble or entice to sin one of these little ones who believes in me, it is better for him that a large grinder-stone be wrapped around his neck, and be thrown into the sea.*** *(Mark 9:36-42 DNT)*

I have been young and now am an aged man,
but I have never seen the righteous destitute,
nor God's children searching for food.

(Psalms 37:25 DOT).

CHAPTER EIGHT

SPIRITUAL PROGRESS PRIORITIES

What are the Priorities?

The first gospel written was the Gospel of Mark. The priority of this Gospel is often neglected because Mark presents Jesus as an active Servant as an example to believers. Forty times Mark wrote that Jesus did this and "straightway" or "immediately" moved to additional action. Mark is a much better place to start reading the Gospel narrative to understand the priority of active service by believers. Luke presents Jesus as a man to a Roman audience to demonstrate human involvement in the divine plan and to show what Christ "began to do and teach." Matthew reviewed the facts that Jesus came through the Jewish Nation to become the Redeemer King. John then puts a cap on the process by declaring Jesus to be Divine the King of Kings, and the Lord of Lords. However, when Mark's presentation of Jesus is understood and followed, believers must be active in serving both God and others. This is the believer's "reasonable service."

The First Commandment

When Jesus was asked which commandment had the first position, Jesus gave precedence to the following:

*29b...The Lord your God is one Lord: 30. And you **shall love the Lord your God with your whole heart, and with your whole existence, and with all your moral understanding, and with all your ability and strength:** 31. namely this, **You shall love as yourself those near you. There is no other commandment greater than these.*** (Mark 12:29 b -31 DNT)

Not only must we see the greatest commandment as a commission to understand the gospel and share the good news, believers must see themselves as valuable in the sight of God, and they must "love" themselves. If one does not see the

130 GOD'S WORK DONE GOD'S WAY

worth and value of their own person, they will not clearly see the value of family, neighbor, or friend. Notwithstanding, the command to love one's enemy and pray for those who despiteful use others including yourself, believers must first give themselves fully to God then share the grace and peace of Christ with others. This is a priority.

First Preach the Gospel to the Nations

A main concern of Christ is that the gospel must be proclaimed first among all nations (Mark 13:10). This primary focus of preaching the gospel certainly hits the current custom of doing most, if not all of the preaching in a church building, rather than out among the people. When the New Testament uses the idea of "preaching" it clearly means what we now call witnessing." The early church did not have buildings in which to worship, and their proclamation of the gospel was in the market place and on the road side: anywhere people would gather or listen. Now some believers look down on the "street preachers" or the risk takers who attempt to carry out the priority of proclamation.

The "Children's Bread"

When the Syro-Phenician woman asked Jesus to heal her daughter, Jesus said let the children first be fed, that it is not right to take the children's bread and to throw it to the house-dogs. She then explained that the dogs eat the children's crumbs, and Jesus responded by healing her sick child (Mark 7:24-30). **The truth of this scripture is that God expects the needs of the believers to be met first; then with all the strength and grace that a healthy and spiritual church can muster, they are to serve the needs of the community.** The "children's bread" is to be shared with those who do not know Christ in the free pardon of sin. First the saints must be fed so they can then share the Bread of Life with the lost. The nature of the present church is to feed the whole loaf to the believers and leave almost nothing for the lost. The saints have first place in receiving the milk of the word, the fruit of the Spirit, and the strong meat of the scripture. Then the strengthened saints must share the children's bread with those who need it most.

First Seek the Kingdom of God

29. And seek not what you shall eat, or drink, neither be disturbed with cares. 30. For all these things do the nations of the world seek after: and your Father knows that you need these things, 31. **But rather seek the kingdom of God and all these things shall be added to you.** *(Luke 12:29 -31 DNT)*

First, Thank God for Faithful Believers

8. **First, I continue to thank my God through Jesus Christ for all of you, because your faith is proclaimed all over the world.** *9. Calling God to witness, whom I serve with my spirit in the gospel of his Son, how spontaneously I always include you in my prayers; 10. making requests that my whole journey to you would be prosperous by the will of God (Romans 1:8-10 DNT).*

First Seek the Welfare of Others

23. All things are lawful for me, but all things are not beneficial. All things are lawful, but all things do not build up the body spirituality. 24. **Let no man seek his own benefit, but every man continually seek the welfare of others.** *(1 Corinthians 10:23, 24 DNT)*

Make Me a Cake, First!

It is easy to see the negative side of things. For example, the church is never half full; it is seen as half empty. This is done without the realization that every empty seat is filled with the presence of God. Believers should never look at a half-full glass, but should always see it filled: half with something and half with air. They should then come to the knowledge that God is spirit and fills the whole world and that the balance of a half-full glass is filled with the spirit and presence of God.

When the day of small things are despised, the larger blessing will be lost. The widow with only and meal enough oil to make a final meal for herself and her son responded to the Prophet's request, **"Make me a cake, first."** Notwithstanding her poverty, she responded to the request of the Prophet, and her meal barrel or her oil pot never went empty during the whole of the famine. The darkest part of the night is just before day break. The hardest part of the hill is just before one reaches the top. God generously rewards those who seek to follow the plan to do God's work God's way, but we must first take the necessary steps with the direction of divine guidance.

A Necessary Step

Understanding that God fills the universe is a necessary step in social or spiritual progress. One should never despise the day of "small things." It was **one small stone** that brought down the Giant Goliath. It was the sight of a **small dove** that made Noah understand that he and his family were safe. It was **a cloud as small as a man's hand** that caused the Prophet to rejoice in deliverance. It was **three small spikes** that nailed Jesus to the Cross, but it was His great love for mankind that kept Him there. He could have called 10,000 angels, but obedience and love produced the necessary sacrifice that brought salvation to the world. It does not take a great leap of faith to decide to assist God's work; it is permitting the Holy Spirit to remove the scales from the eyes so the need can be seen. The God of all creation is very near each of us; if we but reach out, we will feel His Presence and know that we are not alone. In God's work each believer must lead by example. Someone is following you; will they be on the right path?

24. The God who ordered the universe and all the things in it, the One being Lord of heaven and earth does not dwell in hand-made shrines; 25. Neither is he served by human hands, as though he needed something from man, seeing he gives to all life, breath, and all things; 26. And has made of one blood all nations of men who dwell on the earth, determined the history of nations and their territory; 27. **So they should search for God and hopefully find him although he is not far from all of us. 28. For in him we live and move, and have our being;** *(Acts 17:24- 28 DNT)*

Lead by Example

Believers must lead by example in every aspect of life. Individual influence is positive only when others see a good example to follow. Spiritual leadership is to furnish an escort to guide the way forward but also to provide companionship to shepherd others into the green pastures of grace and truth. To stand out front and lead is a place of honor and deserves the respect of all concerned. There was once a young man in church who had very low self-esteem. He felt as though he could do nothing right and had little if any self-worth. One day he was told, "Everyone is good for something!" He responded by asking, "What am I good for?" After some hesitation the adult told the lad, "You are a good bad example, and I am going to show you how to become a good one." This was what he needed to turn his life around. He needed someone to care enough to look him in the eyes and offer personal assistance. This kind of person others will follow.

Follow Me as I Follow Christ

Paul recorded what he told his converts when he wrote, "Follow me as I follow Christ." He led by example. Except when an individual's attitude and acceptance of others becomes child-like, little progress can be made in advancing human relations. Scripture suggested that "even a child shall lead them." Have we not witnessed the action of a small child cause the heart of a hard-hearted person to melt into an affectionate embrace of the child? Also the scripture teaches that "Except we become as a little child, we shall not enter the Kingdom of God." It may be difficult for those who see themselves as leaders in the world or the church to become humble and behave in a way that wins friends and influences people to "follow me as I follow the Lord."

What about you? What kind of example are you? What if every member of the church lived as you do, what kind of church would there be? What if every spouse behaved as you do, would the institution of marriage be better? Remember, someone is watching you. The observation is close and personal and all negative perspectives will be passed on to others. What kind of example are you? You must walk the talk or the negative consequences will impact your life and repetition.

Personal Behavior

To effectively lead one must be an example in all aspects of life. There are no exceptions. "A bird with a broken wing can never fly as high again." Personal behavior can clearly undermine professional accomplishments. All who would be involved in spiritual and/or social change must maintain good behavior and "practice what they teach or preach." They must become a model of Christ-like behavior.

Corrupted by Bad Company

Believers must take care that they do not get pulled down to the level of bad associates. At times to do God's work, believers must associate in the public square with individuals who do not follow faith-based guidelines for their lives. It is easy for bad company to corrupt even believers. Keep a level head, as a right-minded adult should, and do not get drawn into the evil of the crowd. Call on the agency of the Holy Spirit; it is the Spirit that walks with the believer in the world and empowers faith and right behavior. The Spirit also defends as a spiritual attorney a believer against the wiles of the Devil. Keep your mind clear and your eyes fixed on the spiritual prize. Do not be distracted from the purpose for which you were called.

Bad Company

32. If as a man I suffered maltreatment from evil men at Ephesus, **what have I gained if there is no life after death?** *Why not just eat and drink and die? 33.* **Do not permit yourself to be fooled: bad company spoils good behavior.**

34. Come to your senses and stop sinning; *for some of you are truly ignorant of God: I say this publicly to your individual shame. (1 Corinthians 15:32-34 DNT)*

A Model for Believers

6. And you became imitators of us, and of the Master, having accepted the word on a narrow path, but with joy of the Holy Spirit: 7. **So you became a model for all the believers** *in Macedonia and Achaia. 8. For from you echoed out the word of the Master not only in Macedonia and Achaia, but also in every place your trust God-ward is overflowed abroad, so that we do not need to speak a word; 9. For others are telling of their own accord, what welcome you gave us, and how your turned from idols to serve the living and sincere God; 10. And to confidently wait the return of God's Son from heaven, whom he raised from a corpse, even Jesus our rescuer from the coming wrath. (1 Thessalonians 1:6-10 DNT)*

Always follow the Good

12. We request brethren that you know those who labor among you, and are over you in the Lord, and give you special directions; 13. And respect them highly in love for their work sake. And be at peace among yourselves. 14. We urge you, brothers, warn the idle, comfort the faint hearted, support the physically weak, show longsuffering with all men. 15. Be certain that no one retaliates evil for evil to any man; **but always follow that which is good, but among yourselves, and to all men.** *(1 Thessalonians 5:12-15 DNT)*

An Example for You to Follow

1. Finally, brethren, pray for us, that the word of the Lord may hold its onward course and be extolled and triumph, even as it did with you: 2. And that we may be preserved from wrong-headed and malicious men for all men do not have faith. 3. But the Lord is faithful, who shall strengthen you, and protect you from evil. 4. And **we have assurance in the Lord concerning you, sure that you are doing and will do as we instructed you. 5. And may the Lord guide your**

**hearts into a deeper realization of God's love and into
steadfastness as you patiently wait for Christ.** 6. Now we
instruct you, brethren, in the name of our Lord Jesus Christ,
that you shun any brother whose life is disorderly, and not
after the way of life you received from us. 7. **For you know
how you should imitate us: for we behaved ourselves
orderly among you;** 8. Neither did we eat without paying
for it; but toiled hard night and day, that we might not be
a burden to anyone: 9. Not that we did not have the right
of support, **but to make ourselves an example for you to
follow.** (2 Thessalonians 3:1-9 DNT)

God of "Another" Chance

Most of us have had multiple chances to do better or
to correct our behavior. What if we had only one chance to
change, where would we be? There must be a tolerance and an
understanding about human weakness and failure. Once this
is clear it becomes easy to practice the Golden Rule "Do unto
others what you would have them do unto you." Often we are
hard on others when we see our own weaknesses expressed
in their behavior. Memory of our own personal problems can
make us more willing to assist those whose behavior is lack-
ing in maturity. It takes time to grow a child, build a building,
complete a project, or change a community. Patience becomes
a virtue in dealing with the needy. When Paul was nearing the
end of his life he gave John Mark a second chance to participate with him in ministry. Mark had previously deserted Paul
on a missionary journey, but was now seen as being profitable
and useful for the ministry.

John Mark had Another Chance

9. Hasten to come to me shortly: 10. For Demas forsook me,
having loved this present age and went to Thessalonica;
Crescens to Galatia, Titus to Dalmatia. 11. Only Luke is with
me. **Pick up Mark and bring him with you: Mark is useful
to my ministry.** 12. And Tychicus have I sent to Ephesus. 13.
When you come bring the top coat I left at Troas with Carpus,

and bring the scrolls, and especially the rolls of parchment.
(2 Timothy 4:9-12 DNT)

Another Chance after a False Step

1. Brethren, if a man should take a false step due to weakness, you who are spiritual, strengthen and sustain him with a teachable spirit; continue considering yourself, lest you also be tempted to make a false step. *2. Practice in sharing the heavy burdens of others, and you will fulfill the law of Christ. 3. If a man supposes himself to be something when he is really nothing, he deceives himself. 4. Let every man test himself for innocence, and then he shall rejoice in himself and not in another. 5. For every man must carry his own personal load. (Galatians 6:1-5 DNT)*

An Extreme Example of Another Chance

*12. Thanks I give to the one empowering me, Christ Jesus our Lord, because **He deemed me faithful putting me in his service**, 13. Who was a blasphemer, a persecutor, a man of violence, author of outrage, and yet he had mercy on me, because I was acting in the ignorance of unbelief. 14. But the grace of our Lord was more than abundant with faith and love which is in Christ Jesus. 15. What a true saying and worthy of a favorable reception, that Christ Jesus came to the world to save sinners; of whom I rank first. 16. And yet I was pardoned, **so that in me first Christ Jesus might give an extreme example of his longsuffering; I was to be a precedent for** all those who will ever believe in him and win eternal life. 17. Now to the King of the ages, incorruptible and invisible only God, be honor and glory unto the ages of the ages. Amen.*
(1 Timothy 1:12-17 DNT)

In the Image of God

In an interview with Bailey (Christianity Today, March 2011) about his conversion to Christianity from Hinduism, Bobby Jindal, while serving as Governor of Louisiana stated, "We're made in God's Image, and it's tragic that the modern world doesn't take the value of life more seriously." There is but one race: the human race. God has made of "one blood all nations" of the earth. Human beings are all made "in the image of God" and share the common bloodline that reaches from Creation to Calvary. In reality there is no difference based on race or ethnicity when one is dealing with the value of the individual. There may be differences in language, religion, customs, traditions, and appearances, but this does not change the central fact that all human beings share the image of God.

A Personal Deity

Since we were all made in God's image, when each of us looks at God, we must see ourselves. That means God is a personal deity to each one. Each human being may experience this closeness. As we see God we may also recognize those we love, family and friends. As we see their likeness in God, our love should grow. Our love for God should increase our love for family. The word tells us to love even our enemies; perhaps we should be looking in God's face to see if we can see our enemies. It sure would make it easier to pray for them.

Poor Self-Image

Some because of conditions in their family or community develop a poor self-concept, and this produces a weak self-image. Individuals with a poor self-image normally project that faulty image to God and to other human beings. The big question is: have those who do not believe in a personal God projected this construct to their life and to the world at large? If so, has this projection created a secular society without faith-based values? If this be true, what can believers do about this tragic state of affairs?

God is not a Respecter of Persons

God loved the whole world. Jesus went to the Cross of Calvary for all mankind. The Holy Spirit is in the world reproving all of righteousness, sin, and judgment in order that "all should be saved." God is not willing for anyone to be lost. It was not God's plan for anyone to go to hell, because hell was made for the Devil and his angels. However, when human beings refuse to answer the call to salvation they remain on the side of evil, and their lot will be with the lost. God does not pick and choose those He would bless. There are rules and a set of laws that all must follow to inherit eternal life. The call to salvation is there for all. However, when one accepts God's call they are expected to share their faith with others. As they go about their daily lives, the light of God's love will shine on all with whom they come in contact. This is the plan to do God's work God's way.

"The Lord is not slow concerning his promise as some men count slowness; but is longsuffering to all, not wishing any to perish, but desiring all to take the way of repentance,"

(2 Peter 3:9 DNT).

CHAPTER NINE

MARCHING ORDERS: "DO AS YOU GO."

The Primary Task

The primary task of the early followers of Jesus was to make disciples. Jesus instructed them "to wait in Jerusalem" until the Holy Spirit equipped them to go to the whole world with the message of saving grace. The marching orders were "as you go" into all the world make disciples by teaching and baptizing believers. This task was passed on to believers in each generation. As believers matured they joined the expedition to spread the faith in Christ across the known world. The basic instructions of Jesus were grossly misunderstood. Some see the commission as orders to the hierarchies of religion to guide their professional work; others see the commission as only for the New Testament people, but those who experience true conversion and the enabling of the Holy Spirit see Christ's command as a program for people in motion. It is truly a call to lifestyle evangelism. It is not a "go and do" but a "do as you go" concept that guides believers in doing God's work God's way.

Personal Evangelism

The commission is to do personal evangelism "people to people" rather than "pastor/preacher to people." Preaching and teaching on Sunday is more education than it is outreach. In reality the commission is for believers to work in their own environment, in their Jerusalem first, and then go to the surrounding communities, before concentrating on the rest of the world. The church must stop playing leap frog over local community responsibilities and appeasing their conscience by giving a little to foreign missions. Going to the entire world and "taking a picture of every creature" is not the purpose of the commission. Sadly, many of those pictures are shown in local churches to raise money to go back and "do it again" with little evidence of making disciples the first time.

The Plan was Disciple Making

The commission is God's call to all believers to become effective in daily Christian living and witness to everyone they encounter. The plan is simple: as you go, or going into all the world, **make disciples**. This is the objective: to make disciples. When an individual accepts Christ, bring them to a church or faith-based place of worship to be identified with Christ through water baptism and formally introduced to the fellowship of other believers. Through this process they can become exposed to scriptural teachings about living a clean and holy life separated from the sins of the world. In this way they can become a witness to God's saving grace. In sharing the good news with their family and friends, they can enlarge the Kingdom.

People Anxious to Go

The Great Commission was given to believers who were anxious to go and share the good news, but they were told to wait in Jerusalem until they received the power of the Holy Spirit. This empowerment would enable them to go not only in their own strength using their talents, but also go under the authority and in the name of Christ. This would enable them to become true witnesses for the grace of God. Once the power was received they were to go about their daily lives witnessing to all who would listen. It was to be a lifestyle; clearly a "do as you go" process rather than a program of "go and do."

Plan to Equip the Saints

Most of us want to go somewhere and do something when in reality our own environment presents plenty of opportunity for good works. The word of God and the teaching ministry of the local church are to equip believers to share the gospel as they go about their daily lives. Converts should be taught to stay in their own "Jerusalem" until the work of witnessing to family and friends is finished then journey to other areas of need. If everyone worked on family and friends first and those near their own homes, the Nation and God's work would get done God's way. It is the "go and do" mindset that causes us to neglect those closest to us. If you do not reach them...who will?

As You Go

> 19. **As you go to all nations make disciples**, baptizing them to the name of the Father, and of the Son, and of the Holy Spirit; 20. teaching them to observe all things whatsoever I have instructed you. And behold, I am with you all the days, until the end of the age. (Matthew 28:19, 20 DNT)

Wait for the Spirit

> 8. But you shall receive miraculous ability and strength, after the Holy Spirit is come upon you: and you shall be my witnesses unto the death both in Jerusalem, and in all Judaea, and in Samaria, and continually into the farthest part of the earth. (Acts 1:8 DNT)

When Evangelism doesn't Work

When an unconverted individual reaches the sanctuary on Sunday without a true change of heart, it is evidence that the local program of evangelism is not working. Evangelism is basically as believers go into the highways and byways, they bring converts into the house of prayer for baptism and teaching. God's house is not a den of thieves; it is to be filled with converted souls who are seeking closer identification with Christ, spiritual fellowship, and a closer walk with God.

A Field instead of a Force

Evangelism is in reality observing how God is already working in the life of someone through the Holy Spirit and the prayers of others and then acting to meet the person at their point of need. A major difficulty in the outreach perspective about the community is that most believers see their faith-based group as a field to work in rather than a force with which to work to reach the community for Christ and social change. Believers must not limit spiritual activities within the fellowship, but must spread the good news of salvation to their field of influence. The worship experience enables believers to joyfully share their faith with their daily contacts. Believers must not frustrate the grace of God by withholding their personal testimony. It is the force of the personal witness in the field that advances Christianity.

Stuck in Previous Patterns

Tradition and a lazy approach to prayer and scriptural activity have permitted believers to become stuck in previous patterns of behavior. They go to church and feel as if they have done God a service. This attitude causes many to be stuck in the ways of the past with little or no creative ideas or individual initiatives in outreach to meet the needs of individuals in the community. The scriptural injunction is for present action in the field that is ready for harvest. The ways and means of the past may not inform the present needs of the lost. Worship and spiritual fellowship generates the force to go forth and share the good news.

Weak Links in the Chain of Evangelism

When individual believers fail to become active witnesses to the saving grace, they become weak links in the chain of evangelism. Some say a chain is not stronger that its weakest link; however, the breaking of a weak link simply leaves two shorter chains. With this understanding, a weak link will shorten the outreach to the community until a "master link" replaces the weak link in the chain of evangelism and restores the chain to its full length. Prayer, worship, and personal reading of scripture can strengthen a believer to become a strong link in the chain of outreach. Weak links limit the personal witness as weak disciples follow Christ at a distance.

Distant Discipleship

Jesus had told the disciples, "Pray lest you are tempted." Peter was one of the "insiders" who was extremely close to Jesus and listened to His every word. However, it seems that Peter was living beneath his privileged position. Perhaps his **first step backward was a neglect of prayer**. Even in the Garden when Jesus was seeking to conquer the human element so He could submit to the will of God, Peter was part of the inner circle that slept at a crucial time as Jesus prayed. This initiated an attempt to resist the gang arrest of Jesus by physical force. This was his **second step backward** as he hastily substituted angry physical action in response to the arrest of Jesus. After drawing his sword in anger and attempting to cut off the head of the High Priest's servant, Peter had to settle for an ear. Jesus intervened and replaced the ear. This should have been a rebuke, but Peter's negative attitude caused him to ignore this act of mercy. Jesus told him that he would also betray Him three times before the cock crows twice. Peter was becoming a distant disciple and ignoring the obvious slippery slope toward denial.

Growing Spiritually Cold

Peter's **third step backward** was to follow Jesus at a distance and grow spiritually cold. It was his third strike, and Peter was cold enough to warm by the devil's fire and to begin denying that he knew Jesus. This was the opposite of the positive action and witness that had characterized Peter's relationship. This was after his declaration that others may leave the fold, but he declared to stay with Christ even to the death. He said, "Even though, all shall be scattered from you, yet I will not stumble." When the disciples scattered, Peter followed at a distance and warmed by the "devils fire" after repeating emphatically, "Even if I must die with you, God forbid, I will never deny you," (Mark 14:29-31 DNT). This was a sad turn of events for Peter, but Jesus prayed for his restoration and that when he was restored he would "strengthen" the others.

A Sad Turn of Events

Peter's loyalty was based on a personal attachment to Jesus and fellowship with the other disciples. His commitment was to One for whom he was willing to die. Scripture records, "No one can give greater proof of love than giving his life for his friends," (John 15:13 DNT). When Christianity is analyzed it is not a philosophy that one accepts, nor a theory one can validate; it is a personal loyalty to Jesus Christ that one must demonstrate. This creates faithfulness and a fervent love that one gives because the nature of the relationship would not permit anything else.

The Sad Sojourn of Peter

> 66. And as Peter was beneath in the courtyard, one of the maidservants of the high priest came: 67. And when she saw Peter warming himself, she looked closely at him, and said, You also was with Jesus of Nazareth. 68. But he denied, saying, I neither know nor understand what you mean. And he went out to the covered entrance; and the cock crew. 69. And the maid saw him, and began again to speak to the bystanders, This man is one of them. 70. And a second time Peter denied it. Soon after, a bystander said again to Peter, Surely you are one of them: you are a Galilean. 71. But he began to curse and to swear, saying, I know not this man of whom you speak. 72. **And the second time the cock crew.** And Peter remembered the words of Jesus, Before the cock crows twice, you will deny me three times. **And when he thought about those words, he began to sob.** (Mark 14:66-72 DNT)

Jesus Prayed for Peter

Jesus prayed that Peter's faith would not fail. He said, "Simon, Satan has desired to have you that he may sift you as wheat." Jesus knew that Peter would deny Him. Jesus also knew that Peter would repent of his distant discipleship and be restored to a position of leadership among the disciples. Therefore, Jesus told Peter, "When you return to me, strengthen your brethren." Peter had a human failure as many other followers of Jesus have experienced. He also repented with tears and was restored to his former place of honor. This speaks volumes of redemptive hope to all who follow Jesus and have "spiritual failures" along the journey. This means that there is a ministry of reconciliation for all who acknowledge their distant discipleship and desire restoration as a full-time witness to the saving grace of Christ (Luke 22:31, 32 CNT). Reconciliation requires movement on both parties. God reaches His hand to restore; those who falter must take the Hand of God by faith and claim a restored position in Christ.

Apostles of the Streets

God's plan is for all converts to become apostles sent with a message for the streets. Apostle means "sent with a message." Each and every believer, regardless of how they earn a living or the position or role they may serve in the church, is obligated to share the message of God's grace to a lost world. True believers can no longer remain comfortable in a church pew waiting for the unconverted to come into a House of Prayer to hear songs that do not relate to their lives or hear sermons that they do not understand. The lost are blinded and cannot see the light of the gospel that would bring them to salvation. As a burning and shining light, each believer must cultivate access to unbelievers and influence them to follow the light as God illuminates the truth of the Word to their hearts. A failure to use each home as a beacon to a dark world and a signal to the lost that points the way, the homes of believers will never become an extension sanctuary where the lost can find their way to the Cross. In fact, the home of every Christian should be a lamp post glowing in the night, knocking holes in the darkness that keeps individuals from seeing and knowing God's love and saving grace.

Give the Light of Understanding

*1. **Therefore seeing we have this commission, as received by the mercy of God, we do not get discouraged;** 2. But have renounced disgraceful and underhanded ways, we do not practice trickery or adulterate the word of God; only by openly declaring the truth we recommend ourselves to the honest judgment of man in the sight of God. 3. **But if our gospel is veiled, it is veiled to the lost: 4. whose unbelieving minds are blinded by the god of this world, lest the image of God and the glorious light of the gospel of Christ should shine unto them.** 5. For we preach not ourselves, but Christ Jesus the Lord; and ourselves your servants for Jesus' sake. 6. **The same God who caused light to shine out of darkness has caused his light to shine within our hearts, to give the light of understanding of the glory of God in the face of Jesus Christ.*** (2 Corinthians 4:1-6 DNT)

"As you go into all the earth, make disciples, baptizing and teaching...," (Matthew 28:19 DNT).

AMEN!

CHAPTER TEN

CALLED TO BE FAITHFUL

Called to be Faithful

A difficult story is told of a painter working for years on a picture of the Last Supper of Jesus with His disciples. The artist wanted each face to appear authentic. When it came time to put faces into the picture, he found a young man to model the face of Jesus. The face was full of natural beauty and an unexpected loveliness for a man. The artist was satisfied that the face depicted what he wanted to show about Jesus. One by one the face of each disciple was added to the picture. Judas was left for last. In searching for a model for the face of Judas, he went to the slums, among the poorest of the poor, and finally he found a man. The face was marked with pain and a sadistic expression just what he wanted for Judas. When he was about finished with the model, the man spoke, "You painted me before." The artist was shocked and said, "Surely, not!" The response, "I was the model for the face of Jesus." The marks of sin and depravity had etched in the face of this man an unimaginable difference than when he was the model for Jesus.

"Christ-like" or "Judas-like"

Isaiah presented contrasting portraits of Jesus, one as "a tender plant" growing up to become the Messiah, and another looked at the Crucified Christ on the Cross as "having no outward attractiveness and no beauty in appearance that would make one desirable," (Isaiah 53:2 DOT). Perhaps the artist portrait of the Last Supper presented this contrast in the model. As a young man he could model for the face of Jesus, and after a life of degradation, he could become a model for the face of Judas. So it is with those "called to be faithful" and who then live a life that denies a relationship with Jesus. In one picture the believer is "Christ-like." In another portrayal, one may appear as Peter who cursed, lied, and denied Christ, but repented and was restored. Finally, one can have the appearance of a "Judas-like" model whose unfaithfulness had marked a drastically different person. This is a depiction of "best, better, or worst." All who are called have a choice as to how they will be presented to the world. It is best to be Christ-like, but to be repentant as Peter is better than the worst example of Judas.

Called and Sent

All believers are called to be faithful and sent into the world to serve others. Whether they function as a leader in a local congregation or a sales clerk in a downtown store, all are involved in full-time Christian service. How they earn a living is not the issue; ministry requires a daily relationship with Christ and a regular connection with people in need. A confession of sin, a profession of faith, and a personal identification with Christ through the initiation of water baptism are the qualifying elements of the ministry of believers. Ministry is service to others. In reality, to minister is to meet individuals at their point of need at the earliest point in time, at the furthest distance from a place of worship. No scripture requires an individual to come to a house of worship to be converted. They are to be won in the market place where they live and work and then brought to a place of faith-based worship to gain growth in grace and knowledge.

Measure up to God's Standard

God has a standard of faithfulness relative to the attitude and action of believers. Everyone is expected to measure up to God's behavior standard. The Bible standards are available to all who will daily study and behave the Word. That means that believers must walk uprightly before the Lord daily and be a fervent and skilled witness to unbelievers. Believers must measure up to the New Testament standard established by the behavior of the early disciples. They were examples of witnessing first to family and friends: this is friendship evangelism. Then as they moved about the known world, they shared the good news of Christ to all who would listen. As the early believers were guided by the Spirit to share with those God placed in their path, Christianity advanced and became a force in the world. This early faith, enthusiasm, and eagerness to share are missing in the church today. Most believers make little effort toward witnessing to the outside world. They seem to be content to go to church meetings, sing and enjoy the service, say a prayer, and leave without any zeal to share the gospel. Such behavior does not measure up to God's standard of conduct or measure up to a reasonable expectation by the church for outreach.

Fall Short of the Biblical Standards

Consistent positive behavior is the mark of a believer. When believers do not establish a lifestyle that clearly demonstrates their relationship with Christ, they fall short of the biblical standard. When believers fail in daily prayer and a faithful witness to their faith by life and lip, they are moving toward behavior that does not measure up to God's standard. Such failure will ultimately lead to a sinful path. The passive sins of omission are just as damaging to the Christian witness as are active sins of commission. Each sin has consequences.

Faithfulness Produces

In the days of artificial sugar, substitute butter, tofu, and other substitutes for dietary protein, the general public needs people who are true, realistic, authentic, accurate, believable, and true to life. Whether we win the game or are triumphant in a project, it is faithfulness that overcomes life's major difficulties. It is faithfulness that produces positive social and spiritual change. It is faithfulness that produces the wise use of material wealth. The prophet Isaiah wrote about peace and trust,

"You will keep him in flawless peace, whose mind waits on you: because he trusts in you," (Isaiah 26:3 DOT).

A Believer's Legacy

Who we are and what we do may die with us, but those things we can transfer to others becomes our Christian Heritage. What kind of spiritual inheritance will you leave your family and friends? **It is not how or where you die that is important, what will be remembered is how you lived.** Do you walk the straight and narrow way and remain free from the attitude and action that could tarnish your personal reputation and spiritual witness? Do you participate in the religious and spiritual aspects of the church and community? Did you use your time and money wisely? Did you systematically and purposefully pass to others what you had learned and experienced as a believer? You may leave money and property to others in a will, but the primary aspect of a believer's legacy is the spiritual witness that is handed down or remains in the memory and consciousness of those who knew and loved you.

Reproducing Believers

In the law of reproduction, it is clear that each living thing reproduces copies and at time imitations of themselves. The Book of Genesis declared that "the seed is in the fruit." It becomes clear in nature that each plant and animal duplicates a replica. Corn seed produces corn. A tulip bulb generates a tulip. From an acorn an oak tree grows. Monkeys reproduce monkeys, and elephants birth elephants. Therefore, believers should logically reproduce other believers. Reproduction was God's plan in the Garden of Eden as Adam and Eve were told, "Be fruitful and replenish the earth." When Jesus gave His personal commission to believers, they were told to make disciples wherever they journeyed. The big question becomes obvious: what kind of believer can you reproduce? If they are just like you will they be worthy of the name Christian that means "Christ like?" Will your children or those to whom you witness become like Jesus? To be "like" is to be similar or share some of the same features, qualities, or characteristics. What is your record? The growth and the strength of Christianity depends on reproducing believers.

A True Legacy

It has been said that to have a true legacy one must reproduce at least ten (10) living, breathing individuals sufficiently capable of carrying on one's cause, business, or ministry. Why ten copies? It is because the best sometimes fall by the way side and fail to take advantage of their opportunities and carry out their designated task. This means to have a true legacy one must mentor, advise, counsel, guide, and teach many individuals to be sure of producing ten with the same values and objectives you have that can carry on or perpetuate the work you started. No one wants their life's work to be lost because of their passing, but only a few make the effort to produce a true legacy.

Mentoring is not an Easy Task

Discipleship making is similar to mentoring, and it is not an easy task. To adequately disciple and/or mentor an individual is a long and continuous process. It cannot be accomplished in a weekend retreat, a single seminar, a series of workshops, or a casual conversation. It must be scheduled and persistently maintained over time to make certain that both the facts and the heart of the matter is properly implanted in the very core of another. It is a trial and error process. All who start on such a journey will not complete the course. In fact, history shows that most will become bored or somewhat disenchanted with the process and find something more interesting or immediately satisfying. To take over and continue the work and course of another requires a deep motivation that comes from an almost spiritual endowment. It is more spiritual or mystical than it is educational. The persons being mentored must have a committed heart and mind to the process, and the mentor must be consistent and persistent in the process of guiding another to perpetuate a cause, mission, or work.

Faithful Leadership

5. For this reason I left you in Crete, in order that the things wanting you should set in order, and should appoint in each city senior oversight as I had charged you: 6. always looking for one who is beyond reproach, faithful to one woman; one whose children hold the faith, not accused of reckless living. 7. For one who has oversight as the steward of God **must be beyond reproach***, not stubbornly self willed, not easily angered, not given to wine, or one who comes to blows, nor greedy after material gain. 8. But hospitable, a lover of good things, sensible, just, holy, self-controlled, 9. Holding to the faithful word according to the teaching, that he may be able by healthy teaching both to exhort and to convince the contradicting ones. (Titus 1:5-9 DNT)*

Faithful Service Shows Kindness

5. Beloved you are faithfully serving when you show kindness to the brethren, even when they are strangers to you. 6. And they testify of your love before the church: if you send them on their journey as godly men, you do well: 7. because they went out for his name's sake, taking nothing from the Gentiles. 8. It is a duty to support such men, that we may show ourselves fellow workers with the truth. (3 John 1:5-8 DNT)

Faithful Believers are Clear-headed in all Things

1. I charge you before God, and the Lord Jesus Christ, being about to judge the living and the dead at the appearing of his kingdom; 2. Proclaim the word, immediately and at inconvenient times; warn, reprimand, urgently encourage with all longsuffering and teaching. 3. There will come a time when men will not tolerate healthy teaching; but following their own desires shall listen to many teachers because they are impatient to hear something to please and gratify their ears; 4. and they will stop listening to the truth, and be

*turned aside to fictional tales. 5. **You must be clear-headed
in all things, endure hardships, declare the good news,
and fulfill your ministry.** 6. For I am now ready for my blood
to be poured out as a sacrifice, and it is my time to stand
up for departure. 7. I have struggled for the prize, I have
finished the course, I have kept the faith: 8. Hereafter there
is reserved for me a crown of righteousness, which the Lord,
the righteous judge, shall give me at that day: and not only
to me, but to all those who have learned to love his advent.
(2 Timothy 4:1-8 DNT)*

Learned to be Faithful

Through Christ, the Word of God, and the fellowship of
believers we have learned to believe, learned to trust, studied
the Word to learn to be faithful, listened to the preaching-
teaching, and learned to maintain hope and confidence in the
future. Put this all together, and those who have learned these
things have become faithful.   Peter wrote, "Through Him you
have learned to be faithful to God, who raised Him up from the
tomb, and gave Him glory; that your faith and hope might be
centered in God," (1 Peter 1:21 DNT). And that confidence and
hope is centered in God and grounded in fellowship around the
Word.

Faithful Prayer Work

Paul wrote to the consecrated and faithful brethren at
Colosse, "Spiritual blessings and peace from God our Father
and the Lord Jesus Christ," (Colossians 1:1,2 DNT). Paul wrote
further to this same church that their pastor, Ephaphras, was a
servant of Christ and that he was "always doing faithful prayer
work" for them that they would "stand mature and in full assurance and steadfast in the will of God."

Faithful in the Discharge of Duties

Luke wrote about how "fortunate is the servant" that his
Master finds him "faithful in the discharge of duties," (Luke
12:43 DNT). Luke discussed the matter of how those who were

"faithful in small things" could be "trustworthy in big things." Luke continued, "If you have not been faithful in the wealth of this world who will trust you with true riches? And if you have not been faithful with another man's wealth, who shall give you personal possessions?" (Luke 1610-12 DNT). It appears that God's call to faithfulness has consequences relative to leadership roles and personal material possessions. It became clear that believers could not serve God faithfully and also serve the false god of wealth. Those who would be faithful cannot be materialistic.

> *1. This is a faithful saying, if a man desire leadership oversight, he is aspiring to a noble task. 2. One holding an office of watchful care must be scrupulous, faithful to one wife, watchful, sensible, orderly, hospitable, experienced in teaching; 3. Neither intemperate, nor quarrelsome, **free from the love of money;** but gentle, not contentious, **not a craving for possessions;** 4. He must be one who is a good head of his own family, and keeps his children in order by winning their full respect; 5. If a man has not learned how to manage his own household, will he know how to govern God's church? 6. Not a recent convert, lest being puffed up he fall into judgment of the devil. 7. Moreover he must have a good report from those outside the church; that he not fall into reproach and into the snare of the devil. (1 Timothy 3:1-7 DNT)*

Judged to be Faithful to the Lord

When Lydia, a seller of purple from Thyatira, worshipped God and listened to the Disciples preach, "the Lord opened her heart and she gave heed to the words of Paul." She and her household were converted and baptized, and Lydia came to Paul's group and said, "If you have judged me to be faithful to the Lord, come into my my house and abide there." Her conversion and her faithful witness opened the door for the preacher to dwell in her house. This was because of her pressure on Paul's group (Luke 19:14,15 DNT). The early disciples lived by a creed that was an affirmation of faith.

THE APOSTLES' CREED

I believe in God the Father Almighty,
Maker of heaven and earth:

And in Jesus Christ His only Son, our Lord; who was conceived by
the Holy Spirit, born of the Virgin Mary, suffered under Pontius
Pilate, was crucified, dead, and buried; He descended into Hades;
the third day He rose again from the dead; He ascended into
heaven, and sitteth on the right hand of God; the Father Almighty;
from thence He shall come to judge the quick and the dead.

I believe in the Holy Spirit, the holy Christian church, the
communion of saints, the forgiveness of sins, the resurrection of
the body, and the life everlasting.
Amen.

"Now unto him that is able to keep you from slipping, and to present you blameless before the presence of his glory with exceeding joy, to the only wise God our Savior, be glory and majesty, dominion and power, before time was, and now, and for all ages. Amen!" (Jude 24, 25 DNT).

CHAPTER ELEVEN

BROKEN LIVES — BETTER LIVES

A Few did so Much

Many years before Churchill wrote "Never has so many owed so much to so few" as a tribute to the efforts of a few RAF airmen to save England from German bombers, it was recorded that deep in Church history 75 German Christians in 1727 were praying when the Holy Spirit fell on them, and the Moravian revival began. It has been suggested that those few German believers did more evangelistic and missionary work in a few years than all the churches did in 200 years. This revival touched Charles and John Wesley. After Charles's deeper experience of faith and commitment, they were aboard ship during an Atlantic storm in 1735. The only passengers who were not afraid were a group of singing Moravians. John Wesley wanted to know why they were singing instead of praying. They responded, "If God wills that we go down in this storm, we will have instant entrance into Glory." When John spoke to the leader further, he wanted to know what they had that he didn't have. The answer was "grace."

Something was Missing

John realized that something was missing in his spiritual life and asked if the leader thought he should stop preaching. The wise leader said something similar to this, "When you understand grace, preach it because you have it, but first preach grace because it is in the Bible." The makeover of John Wesley and his ministry is now well known. When the missionary witness of a few German Moravians is traced through history, one finds the foundation stones of Methodism, the Salvation Army, and the early Spirit-filled Movement. These movements brought the work of the Potter in remaking good believers into better saints. These makeovers bring me to the story of the Potter's House.

The Message of the Potter's House

God spoke to Jeremiah, "Arise, and go down to the potter's house, and I will enlighten you on my word." He went to the potter's to learn the lesson of the clay. When Jeremiah arrived at the potter's house, the potter was working on the wheel, and the vessel he was making became marred. So the Potter made the clay into another better vessel (Jeremiah 18:1-10). Is this not the message to each of us who were marred by sin, and the Master Potter made us over again into a vessel of honor? This is what the Second Birth is all about. Believers are to be an honorable vessel in the service of the Lord. In the hands of the Master Potter each convert has a chance to become a better believer and be more committed to the cause of Christ.

The Lesson of the Potter's House

All must learn the lesson of the Potter's House. Regardless of where one visits a Potter's Shop, they are all the same: there is always a potter, lumps of clay, and a turning wheel. Also, there are a few pots around the shop, and some are better than others. One should read Matthew 27: 1-10 to understand that the betrayal price of Jesus was used to buy a Potter's Field. This was to be a burial ground for criminals, paupers, the unknown and friendless people, and the broken ones the Master Potter came to remold into a better image. The price that delivered Jesus to the Cross not only purchased salvation for a lost world, but also brought a Potter's Field for all the rejected and broken pots of humanity.   Perhaps this is the strongest message that the death of Jesus was directly related to the downtrodden, the rejected, and the discarded broken pots. Perhaps we were all broken pots. The story of the Potter's House has four parts: the principle, the purpose, the process, and the person.

Principle and Purpose

The **principle** or basic assumption is that God is the Potter, and He is the controlling factor in the process. The **purpose** is the general direction that God is pointing believers to the high road that leads to life eternal. It is easy to see that the Potter's purpose is to fashion human beings into vessels of honor fit for the Master's use. This requires making an individual into an original vessel in the image of God. Remember, at Creation God said, "Let us make man in our image." Sin and wickedness has marred the clay image, and the Master Potter has as His purpose to remake each one into a proper vessel that carries the spiritual essence of God. "Therefore if a man cleanses himself from the dishonor, he shall become a vessel of honor, set apart and suitable for use by the master, having been prepared for every good work," (2 Timothy 2: 21 DNT).

Process and Person

When the purpose is understood, the basic assumption becomes clear: God is in charge of the process. The **process** is the action used by the Potter to create a new vessel. We are the clay on the potter's wheel. The potter squeezes the clay to get all the air and foreign particles out that could be a blemish on the completed vessel. The clear process is that the potter works patiently and personally on one lump of clay at a time. In other words, each one of us is given personal attention. The clay is worked with the potter's hands to press and stretch the clay until it is a smooth and uniform lump before the clay is placed on the potter's wheel. **Perhaps this process is the daily circumstances of life that God uses to shape us into what He wants us to become.** This shaping of the clay is the process of making a believer into a **Person** who is the image of God. Paul was clear that daily he had to crucify the flesh and permit himself to be molded with the Master's hands. The potter reverses the human trend toward degradation and remolds the clay to fit the pattern. Finally the potter looks at the Model, in this case the Person of Jesus Christ, to make certain that each copy has a traceable resemblance to Christ.

Mold Me and Make Me after Thy Will

The first verse of an old consecration hymn written by Adellaide A. Pollard based on Isaiah 64:8 acknowledged that we are the work of God's hand and clearly recognizes Father God as the Potter and the believer as the clay. The verses of "Have Thine Own Way, Lord" were sung many times in worship, but less in recent years. Perhaps there is less consecration where believers are willing to permit God to do His work His way.

Have Thine own way, Lord,
Have Thine own way!
Thou art the Potter, I am the clay.
Mold me and make me after Thy will,
While I am waiting yielded and still.

-- Adellaide A. Pollard

No Happenstance with God

God is in control, and nothing happens without His knowledge. There is no happenstance with God. In the parable of the hidden treasure, it is suggested that God paid the price for the field to get the treasure that was in it (Matthew 13:44). Paul claimed the Potter had absolute control, "Shall the molded clay say to the potter who formed it, why have you made me this way? Has not the potter absolute power over the clay, of the same lump to make one vessel for noble use and another for common use?" (Romans 9:20, 21 DNT). The Master Plan surely related to Jesus being the Master Potter to make the earthen vessels into the image of God, even the broken pots. Among the gifts that God gave to the church were individuals who could "perfect the saints for the work of the ministry." The challenge now is for believers to remember their broken state and how the Potter made them over. Now it is time for us to look beyond the broken pots and see the Master Potter at work.

The Challenge of Broken Lives

Look beyond the challenges of broken lives to the potential for a better life. When people are out of order and their lives are not working, someone must step in to put the pieces together again. Often broken lives are similar to Humpty Dumpty where all the Kings men could not put things together again. But we are not the men and women of an earthly king; we work together with a Heavenly King who has the power to mend broken hearts, to put the pieces of a broken life together, and to make it better than before. We just need to recognize this partnership and be open to the power and work of the divine in making a better life for those in need.

Needy People are Close

Look around you; there are needy people in close proximity to you. We must observe the whole community and assess the areas of concern. What about the community infrastructure? Are all the necessary aspects functioning such as healthcare, schools, non-government organizations, faith-based centers of operation, necessary businesses, adequate transportation, sufficient police protection, and a stable political force? Jesus proclaimed His mission and later said, "As the Father sent me into the world, so send I you!" The contract was sublet to believers. Each one of us must do what we can to make the community and all those who live and work there efficient and effective. Perhaps we should listen more closely to the words of Jesus and **proclaim a year-long effort** to produce sufficient change in individuals, families, faith-based groups, NGO's, and the government itself to improve the lives and living of all. Particular attention must be paid to children, the elderly, the widows, and women who are alone.

*16. And Jesus came to Nazareth, where he had lived as a child: and, as **his custom was, he went into the synagogue***

on the Sabbath day, and stood up to read Scriptures.
17. And they gave him the scroll of the prophet Isaiah.
And unrolling the scroll, he found the place where it was
written, 18. The Spirit of the Lord is upon me, and has
consecrated me to tell glad tidings to the destitute; "to heal
the brokenhearted" and sent me to proclaim deliverance to
the captives, and the recovering of sight to the blind, and to
set at liberty the downtrodden, 19. ***To proclaim a year when***
men can find acceptance with the Lord. *20. And rolling up*
the scroll he gave it again to the attendant, and set down,
and the eyes of the whole synagogue were firmly fixed on
him. 21. And he began speaking, ***Today while you were***
listening this scripture is fulfilled. *(Luke 4: 16-21 DNT)*

Childcare is Close to the Heart of God

Childcare has been close to the heart of God since Jesus gathered the children close to Himself and said, "Except you become as a little child, you may not enter the kingdom of heaven." Since the Garden of Eden, morality has been controlled by females. Why? It is because most women have the grace and strength to resist the immoral pursuits of men. It has been said, "Ten bad men may not corrupt the morals of one good woman; but one immoral woman can corrupt 100 men." Paul, in writing to the Corinthian church, made it clear that a believing spouse must separate an unbelieving spouse from sexual encounters outside of marriage. Paul's determination was that sexual expression outside of wedlock would produce defiled (1 Corinthians 7:14). Could this be the explanation for the corrupt generation that exists in communities around the world? Could this be the reason for organized childcare efforts in an attempt to "restore" abused and abandoned children? Is this the reason for remedial parenting and care for the abuse, neglected, and abandoned? Children are gifts from God and should be appreciated and valued as God's promise for the future.

A Child is a Gift from God

The writer of Psalms understood the value of families, cities, and especially the children and what these meant to a father. The Psalmist wrote, "Unless the Lord builds the house, the workers labor in vain and unless the Lord keeps the city, the watchman works in vain." He continued, "Children are a heritage of the Lord; and the fruit of the womb is God's reward. As weapons are in the hand of a mighty man; so are children of the youth. Happy is the man that has his house full of them," (Psalms 127:1-5). Since children are so valued by God, why do some fail to have the "natural affection" that even the animal kingdom has for their young? When the dumb animals of the earth behave better as parents than some, what does this say about the human race? According to the Psalmist, the power to procreate is God's reward for male and female living together in unity; it is for the continuation of the human race. It is normal to desire to have children.

The Coat-Making Business

The story of Hanna provides an example of a good mother who was "fervent in prayer" and obedient and consistent in worship and was devoted to her family. In 1 Samuel 2 there is a record of Hanna's song of triumph as she pledged to conse-crate her son to life-long service of God. After Samuel was committed to the Temple ministry, his mother visited regularly year by year as he grew. He wore a sleeveless, apron-like garment extending to the hips and was the exclusive coat of the priest when officiating before the altar. Scripture records, "Moreover, his mother made him a little coat, and brought it to him from year to year, when she came up with her husband to offer the yearly sacrifice," (1 Samuel 2: 18, 19). Hanna was in the coat-making business; this was continued prayerful concern for the child as he grew into manhood. Hanna is the example of age-specific care for children as they develop.

166 GOD'S WORK DONE GOD'S WAY

Substitute Parenting

To save some of the defiled generation, charity and faith-based groups are investing both time and energy (and funds) in **a new kind of coat-making business**. Now, the coat-making business has become the remedial and substitute parenting of charity supported and faith-based childcare facilities. This is an effort to redeem and restore the beauty and peace of childhood to neglected, abused, and abandoned children. It is a difficult but essential way to follow the example of Jesus and "struggle to bring the children to Him." It is an expensive and perhaps a second-class way to bring children into adulthood as productive and useful moral citizens. It is a remedial and restorative way to bring healing and hope to children without adequate parenting. It is a way to do God's work God's way.

Honoring Parents is an Obligation

Care and honor for elderly parents is a basic obliga-tion of life and is clearly presented in both the Old and New Testaments as a sacred duty (Deuteronomy 5:16; Matthew 15:4-9). However, when one chooses to neglect the needs of children, they will most likely abandon the child's mother, and ultimately neglect the care of their own elderly parents. The scripture is clear that adult children owe a debt of honor to their parents, and this includes both respect (to look at and pay attention to), and tribute, which is a payback or a "duty obliga-tion" for the investment in time and energy parents made in the upbringing and care of the family.

Responsible Adult Behavior

An adult offspring could never repay parents for the cost of feeding, clothing, housing, and educating them. It is responsible behavior to look after and care for elderly parents. In Jewish times, adults would place their funds in a "kind of savings idea" in reference to the Temple to avoid spend-ing money on their parents. Then when the parents passed, they would retrieve their savings and use it for themselves.

It may be different now, but the attitude and action is similar when one observes the needy elderly and ignores their needs. This happens in spite of the prosperity of their children. The Scripture below points out that to neglect elderly and needy parents is "making the word of God of none effect through tradition." To neglect elderly parents is a travesty before God. There are always consequences when one violates God's plan. What if only the sinners reproduced and the believers remained childless, what kind of world would this be in one generation?

> 9. Full well **you reject the commandments of God, that you may keep your own tradition.** 10. For Moses said, Honor your father and mother; and, Whoever speaks evil of father or mother, let him be executed: 11. **but you say, If a man shall say to his father or mother, it is Corban, that is to say, a gift to the temple, of all the support they might have gained; he shall be free.** 12. **And you permit him to do nothing more for his father or his mother;** 13. **making the word of God of none effect through your tradition....** (Mark 7:9-13 DNT)

Neglect of Parents is a Mockery

Neglect in the name of religion is a mockery before God. The Talmud recorded that the Jews would often make rash vows without the intention of keeping them. The reprehensible practice of adult children avoiding responsibility for the needs of parents was clearly observed in the time of Jesus. Adults would tell their parents that all funds were dedicated to a sacred purpose. This absurdity was utilized as if caring for one's parents was not a sacred task. Jesus called attention to this travesty to show the disregard of a clear commandment of God: the one requiring children to honor and respect their father and mother.

Networking for Community Needs

A community is a group of people in a single neighborhood who have a common identity and share similar experiences. Normally, a public community consists of all ages from the newborn to the elderly. To adequately network for the benefit of the community, the entire scope of the community must be observed and evaluated: the infrastructure and services, the buildings and the people, and the families and the needs of children including the elderly.

THE NEEDS OF THE COMMUNITY

Claim the Community for Christ

Sometimes the church leapfrogs over the community to provide for mission projects elsewhere. There are two areas believers should "claim" for their community. First, claim the territory where God has placed their family and give priority to that community. Then claim the blessings of God for the community and give first place to your Jerusalem.

> *26. And has made of one blood all nations of men who dwell on the earth, determined the history of nations and their territory; 27. So they should search for God and hopefully find him although he is not far from all of us. 28. For in him we live and move, and have our being; as certain also of your own poets have said, For we are also his offspring. (Acts 17:26-28 DNT)*

> *14. For we are not over stretching our commission when we count you in our territory, because our preaching came as far as you with the gospel of Christ; 15. We are not boasting of things built by other men's labor;* **but having increased hope that our labor shall be enlarged through your growing faith and will increase our influence abundantly, 16. to preach the gospel to the Gentiles in the regions beyond you without crossing into another man's carefully marked territory.** *(2 Corinthians 10:14-16 DNT)*

Steps to Opening a Community

There are seven steps to opening a community to social and spiritual improvement. Be certain there are **open highways** to make access to faith-based groups and to make the ministry convenient. There must be **open hands** that do community acts of kindness every day. The love of God and spiritual compassion can **open homes** to serve as extension sanctuaries. This should **open hearts** as a response to love and kindness. Finally, prayer and generous gifts can open heaven and bring showers of blessings from the **open windows** of heaven.

A Simple Plan Called C. A. K. E.

People are sick of words; they want deeds. The current attitude is, "We don't care how much you know until we know how much you care." **OPERATION: C. A. K. E.** will provide an opportunity to clearly demonstrate a real concern for the community. Who could turn down a homemade cake provided by a loving church and a friendly person? The children will love it, and the adults will appreciate the gesture. Even the old folk enjoy a homemade cake; it makes them remember mama and grandma. This is good. Meaningful memories are precious.

Community **A**cts of **K**indness **E**veryday **(C. A. K. E.)** will demonstrate genuine concern for the community and provide an action program to get individuals involved. Organize a faith-based group to operate **C. A. K. E.** Each week have individuals bake seven cakes. Sunday, Monday, Tuesday, and Wednesday cakes should be brought to a faith-based center for delivery to un-churched homes in the community. Cakes for Thursday, Friday, and Saturday should be brought to a designated place each Wednesday for distribution on Thursday, Friday, and Saturday.

Leaders of the group should seek the assistance of other believers to identify needy and un-churched individuals and families, particularly new families to the community. The leader should select a family in the community for each day of the week and deliver the MONDAY CAKE to the Monday Family, etc.

Material about **OPERATION: C. A. K. E.** should be prepared and given to the family with the cake delivery. This material should express the love and concern of local faith-based groups for the community and the families there. Material listing the Services and special programs such as Brotherhood Events, Women's Projects, VBS, Annual Homecoming, Scheduled Revivals, etc. should be included along with the names and telephone numbers of church leaders: Pastors, Deacons, Sunday School Teachers, etc.

The leader should complete a census type form for the household and issue a standard invitation for church attendance. If the family is totally un-churched or has special needs, the visitor should ask permission for the **C. A. K. E** family to initiate follow-up by the appropriate people.

OPERATION: C. A. K. E. will open the doors of seven community homes each week and provide an opportunity to bring a gift cake to the families. In one quarter (13 weeks) this would open about 90 homes and provide a good start in opening the community. Go first to needy and un-churched families and then to the rest of the houses in the community.

In addition to the formal project of seven cakes each week, the people involved in **C. A. K. E.** should be encouraged to seek to find ways to demonstrate acts of kindness every day. What about helping a widow repair a screen door or a leaky roof? Perhaps the teens could pick a family to help out with lawn care because the family cannot get to it for whatever reason (sickness, working late, parents working, no lawnmower, etc.). What about taking flowers to a home where there is sickness or some kindness during the death of a family member? What about offering a "Mothers Day Out" or invite the father to a "fishing trip" or other outing with the Brotherhood? I am confident that good people can come up with many other "good acts of kindness" for every day of the week.

THE NEEDS OF CHILDREN

Damage the children – desecrate the family!
Corrupt the family – destroy the nation!

Anapausis **D**evelopment **A**nd **P**rogram **T**eam
A. D. A. P. T.

The Government of Trinidad and Tobago has adopted parts of the
A.D.A.P.T. program. You may find it at
http://www.moe.gov.tt/about_vision.html

A. D. A. P. T. has suggested a vision for the children of
Trinidad and Tobago. It is a general program of juvenile social-
ization with committed service providers and volunteers who
supply the care, nurture, education, and skills training needed
to gain the age-specific development necessary to function
adequately and make the nation a safe society for children to
live and grow.

A policy is answers worked out in advance to anticipated
questions. Here are some questions that should be answered:

- What role does common sense play in childcare and
  development?

- Could inherited traits and genes explain a child's bad
  behavior?

- What about the home environment or the care by a
  nuclear or extended family?

- Does the normal response to external stimuli (environment) explain a child's behavior?

- How does personal or internal motivation affect child
  performance?

- Where do selfish actions and/or aggressive behavior
  originate?

- Does a caregiver have the potential to undue or over-write the past negative programming of a child and thus affect a more productive future?

- Do children have control over the acts that determine their future? If not, who does?

- What about the impact of character and spiritual formation and external intervention on child development?

- How long does it take to turn a child around after a bad environment?

- Who can and will do the remedial and surrogate parenting?

- What is the general and specific policy for child development in Trinidad and Tobago?

Guidelines for Program Development for Children

- Create an environment conducive to learning that promotes growth, mutual respect, and trust among children and adults.

- Structure programs to educate and develop children giving priority to behavioral and learning needs.

- Provide structures, learning resources, technology, and processes designed to motivate and engage children in learning activities of development to prepare them for the real world of work and family.

- Develop a tutoring/learning process that permits self-directed, individualized, face-to-face, and classroom learning in real life situations with dialog/support systems and technology suitable for growing and developing children.

- Strive for multicultural awareness with a broad exchange of teaching/learning experience across cultural and ethnic boundaries.

- Partner with business and industry to produce meaningful programs for education and development of children.

- Work with the Government and Child Protection Agencies to establish quality programs to meet the needs of neglected children.

Results of Brainstorming about the Needs of Children

1. **Children who can achieve their potential:**

   - Can function with a purpose based on values

   - Can understand their career and vocational pathway

   - Are able to cope with daily challenges

   - Are productive achievers

   - Can function at their best

   - Can use God-given talents to an advantage

2. **Children who are adequately developed socially and culturally:**

   - Are productive and have good self-image

   - Are confident and strong among their peers

   - Are adequately developed socially

   - Are patriotic and courageous in civic affairs

   - Are capable of functioning with moral character in their culture

   - Are developed with interpersonal and language skills

   - Are environmentally aware

- Are desirous to lead and have governance skills
- Are spiritually aware and able to manage conflict
- Are humanely aware of the less fortunate and disadvantaged
- Have an honest sense of family and community
- Are historically aware and capable of foreign interaction

3. **Children who are adequately prepared educationally:**

- Are age-specifically prepared to participate in society
- Are academically balanced to be productive
- Are skilled in critical thinking and problem-solving
- Are prepared to use current technology and the Internet
- Are adequately developed neurologically to overcome learning, speaking, hearing, focusing, and memory or mobility challenges

4. **Children who are healthy and growing normally:**

- Are secure and safe in their home, school, and community
- Are physically fit, mentally alert, well nourished, and psychologically sound
- Are active in exercise, sports, and recreation
- Are capable of wholesome interaction with peers
- Are morally prepared for a productive life

5. **Children who are emotionally mature and happy:**

- Are able to enjoy daily life, have fund and fun, and express happiness

- Are participants in entertainment and celebration

- Are established in their peer group and satisfied with their life

- Are mature and able to become a full-fledged, productive citizen

- Are proficient and able to cope with daily conditions

- Are skilled in finding a safe place to think and grow

- Are capable of finding assistance if they are abused or neglected

- Grow and develop in known stages

Developmental Stages from the Womb

1. Womb to age 3 – period of human bonding.

Remedial bonding is a special intimacy that develops between a surrogate caregiver and a child.

2. Womb to age 5 – elements of personality.

Personality has elements of character, behavior qualities, and expressions of individuality and is recognizable soon after birth. It is the totality of one's attitudes, interests, physical behavioral patterns, emotional responses, social roles, and other individual traits that endure over time. Many scholars agree that (1) temperament, and (2) environment are influential in the development of human personality. Temperament depends on genetic factors and is often called <u>nature</u>, while the environment is called <u>nurture</u>.

3. Womb to age 7– deposits for a knowledge base.

The knowledge base is made up of the short-term memory of facts, information, and data that is used to create the long-term memory that produces competency based knowledge that is relatively permanent. At age 7 or about the time a child enters the third year of school, the foundation baseline should be established; that is, they should be able to read and write at an appropriate level in order to proceed higher in the educational structure.

4. Womb to age 9 – steps in character.

Character is the set of affective, cognitive, and behavioral patterns gleaned from life experience that determines how one thinks, feels, and behaves. Character continues to develop throughout life, although much depends on inborn traits and early childhood experiences. Character is also related to the level of moral development.

5. Womb to age 11 – steps in spiritual formation.

Just as all the other steps in development, spiritual formation begins before birth and continues through about age eleven. Spiritual formation is influenced by significant events in the life of the child, personal experiences, parental and adult behavior, observation of peers, and social changes in or near their early environment.

6. Age 12 – 14 – influence of peers

Among the most destructive things that can happen to a child is to become socially involved with peers who have bad habits, immoral behavior, and weak character. In the general population it is difficult to restrict these associations because the restriction has the reverse effect. This means that the associates of children and adolescents must be monitored and each negative incident promptly dealt with by a loving parent. This is where the custodial environment has an advantage.

7. Age 15 – 18 – influence of other adults

Other adult role models such as teachers, the parents of peers, etc. begin to have significant influence. What custodial care plans to do to prepare children for the real world must be done prior to age 15 or a new and special program must be established to deal with the adolescent behavior.

8. Age 19+ -- second chance to guide conduct/career

By age 19 young people have learned the cost of going to school, driving a car, or living in their own place. They often return to those who raised them for assistance with school or living expenses. This should not be discouraged. It provides a "second chance" to influence their future. See this second chance as an opportunity and an obligation. It is probably the last chance the family of a custodial caregiver will have to influence and guide the young person before they take a permanent place in society. Be positive. Philosophy taught that one could never reach a positive conclusion beginning with a negative premise. The old proverb "accentuate the positive and eliminate the negative" is still a good contribution to child development.

Seeds of Hope

Bridge of Hope has been in operation along the Eastern seaboard of Trinidad changing standards of living since 1998. As part of its community outreach program, Bridge of Hope and the Kernahan Community have partnered with BPTT, COCAL Estate, and SERVOL, in initiating the Kernahan Centre for Community Development (KCCD). This project is in an effort to address some of the needs in that community. Our pioneer programs at the centre have been a Preschool, Video Production Training for youths, Parent Outreach Programs, and Adult Literacy Classes.

Vision for the Bridge of Hope

The vision for Bridge of Hope included a capacity not only for basic childcare, but also residential quarters for the children with shared bathrooms instead of communal facilities, a preschool, a special education school, an images skills program, a multipurpose hall, quarters for staff, dining facilities, playground, common areas, and special training space. Achievements attract attention, and when a project does well, it recommends itself to would be supporters. A vision is more caught than taught. The total budget for the new project was in excess of five million TT dollars or about 850,000 USD.

Corporate and Private Citizens Assisted

Such a project cannot be completed by one or two; many corporate and private citizens came alongside us. The Board of Directors came up with a strategy that we should challenge individuals and companies to cover the cost of a child's room. They were the first to support this plan and other private citizens came alongside, and enough funds were raised to complete the project in 12 months. This was accomplished because we had confidence in God's provision.

Confident in God's Provision

The House of Marketing, Ltd. invested a sizeable amount by faith even though the funds were not available at the time of the pledge. With full confidence that God would provide, the company increased sales by 25% with only a small increase in expenses, and the pledge was covered without any frustration. The key principle is simple, "When you take care of God's business, He will take care of yours." One should never be afraid to step out in faith and do what God calls or impresses should be done.

THE NEEDS OF THE ELDERLY

A philosophy of life in relation to the Elderly must include a positive attitude that values and informs both policy and practice in response to the events and quality of life for senior citizens. This cannot be left to government agencies alone; there must be lay involvement to assure compassion and to put a human face on the process. Life in this regard could mean:

Lay

Involvement

For

Elderly!

<u>With a positive philosophy of life, the elderly would have:</u>

Perspectives on life with

Healthy consequences

Including attitude and behavior

Looking to the future with

Optimism and

Security with

Opportunities and

Plans for

Happy

Years ahead!

With the plans for Olive's House and the complex for the Elderly, senior citizens would have an opportunity for a hopeful future and the quality of life deserved by our parents and those who sacrificed to grow their families and build a moral country.

L.I.F.E. in this context could mean:

Living a good healthy life.

In a safe community environment

Full of social and recreational activities

Especially designed for the elderly

HEALTH + HAPPINESS + HOUSING

H. O. P. E.

Health Opportunities Prepared for Elderly

In addition to the aches and pains of aging, the elderly face a growing list of health issues. Below are some of those frequently reported among the elderly. Managed health care is a goal of all facilities for the elderly.

- Alzheimer's & Dementia
- Ambulatory Difficulties
- Anger
- Cancer
- Depression
- Diabetes
- Diverticulitis
- Hearing Loss
- Heart Disease
- Incontinence
- Intellectual Function
- Lung Disease
- Memory Loss
- Nutritional Deficiency
- Osteoporosis
- Parkinson's Disease
- Vision and Hearing Disorders

H. O. P. E.

Happiness Opportunities Prepared for Elderly

Influencing Happiness for the Elderly

Building healthy and happy communities for active aging adults includes more walking space, green spaces, bike trails, and sidewalks. Enlarged signage is welcomed as well as a wheelchair accessible trail system and a fitness centre suitable for all abilities. The elderly gradually begin to lose functioning ability or have other health issues and usually require assistance as they grow older. The secret to happiness for most elderly is for them to remain in a home-style situation that simulates their own living quarters. Using key pieces of furniture and family pictures are important. The thought of moving from the familiarity of their homes and switching to a strange place creates an unhappy person.

Although one cannot generalize from the results the happiness of all the elderly, past studies found that formal education, geographical areas, and gender can influence happiness. As the population ages, the need for elderly friendly accommodations become increasingly important. The goal for all elder care facilities should be to build a healthy community to insure a happy aging experience. Facilities are designed to cut down on commutes and environmental harm, preserve open space, encourage community collaboration, and mix land uses.

Happiness for Seniors include:

- Keeping in touch with family and friends

- Feeling safe and secure

- Having adequate medical care

- Enjoying a balanced diet

- Having adequate physical therapy and exercise

- Remaining useful

- Reunions with children, grandchildren

- Receiving cards and letters from family and friends

- Enjoying a Birthday Cake

- Interacting with children and young people

- Maintaining their religion faithfully

- Sharing with others their life experience

H. O. P. E.

Housing Opportunities Prepared for Elderly

THE VISION of Olive's House is to create a retirement community that redefines the philosophy of life for the elderly citizens of Trinidad and Tobago so that they feel connected, respected, and encouraged to live a life full of meaning and hope.

In the past two decades, the elderly population has increased in Trinidad and Tobago, and a specific government policy is needed to meet this growing need of senior citizens. The elderly population is expected to grow exponentially in the coming decade. This is both a political and social concern.

Housing Opportunities Prepared for Elderly will be developed in four stages: 1. Residential Facility Housing for able-bodied couples and the ambulatory elderly; 2. Assisted Living Facilities for those who cannot live alone; 3. Skilled Senior Care Facility for seniors who need daily observation and a medical watch; and 4. A Hospice-type facility for the terminally ill.

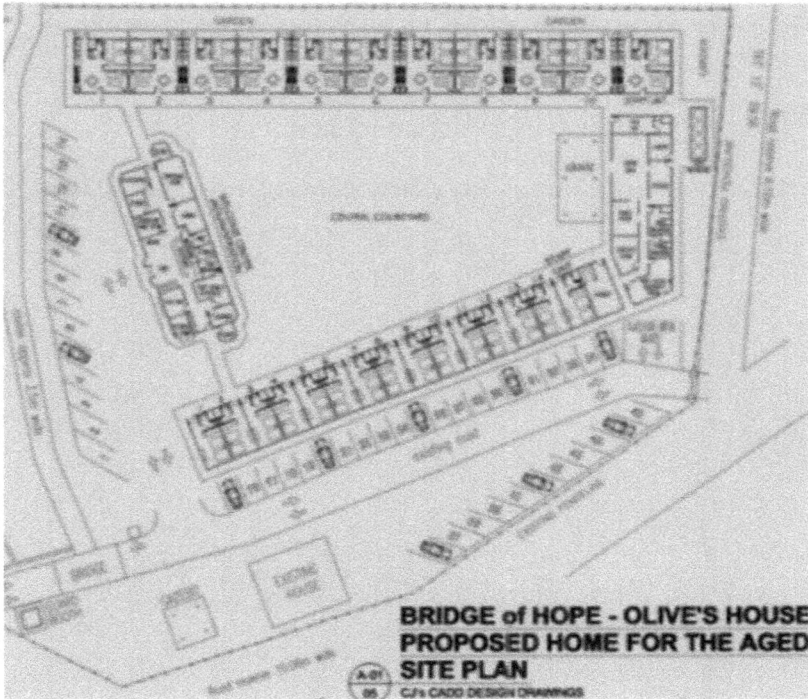

BRIDGE of HOPE - OLIVE'S HOUSE
PROPOSED HOME FOR THE AGED
SITE PLAN
CJ's CADD DESIGN DRAWINGS

STAGE ONE

Housing for able-bodied couples and the ambulatory elderly.

(Residential Facility)

Olive's House as a part of **PROJECT: H. O. P. E.** seeks to provide housing for the post-poverty/pre-middle class poor. This elderly group is in the middle of the low-to-moderate-income group, not specifically classified by the government, but is composed of hard working persons who paid taxes, raised a family, and now their pensions are not sufficient to provide affordable, safe, and age-specific housing for their declining years.

The average elderly person living on a pension does not have a home and is often forced to live with family or children.

These persons cannot afford a condo, a retirement village, or rent for a decent housing opportunity.

OLIVE'S HOUSE

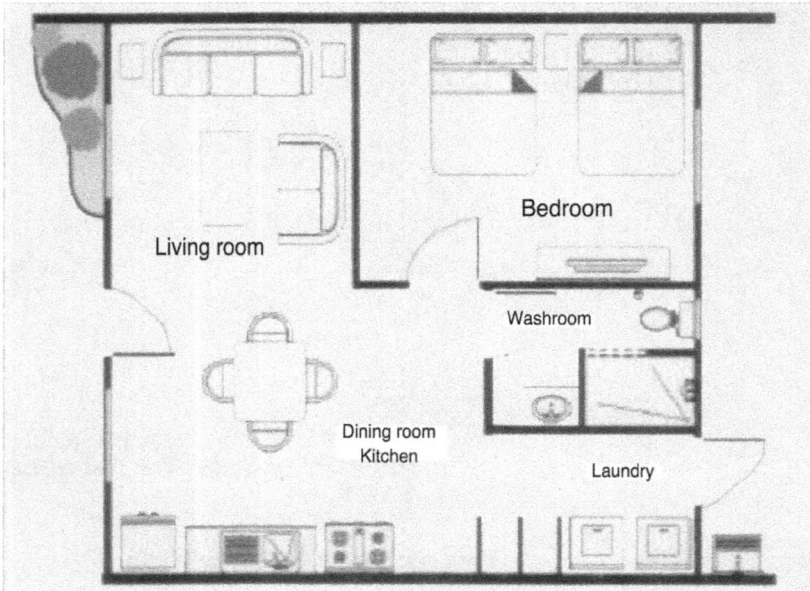

Olive's House is a pilot project that proposes to build 24 ft x 24 ft units on a site in proximity to the Bridge of Hope as a model for senior housing (See Image). These seniors could live on the property as their home as long as one of the husband/wife team is able to function as the caregiver.

STAGE TWO

Assisted Living Facilities for those who cannot live alone.

The elderly are prone to accidents and at times cannot live alone. Others are unable to do basic housekeeping, cook, shop for groceries and need a helping hand. Most cannot afford a live-in companion or a regular nurse so they must move to assisted living or become a burden to their family. Often their mate has passed, and the children live away or have migrated. There is a growing need for a facility designed to assist these seniors with the basic care they require.

A single floor-plan

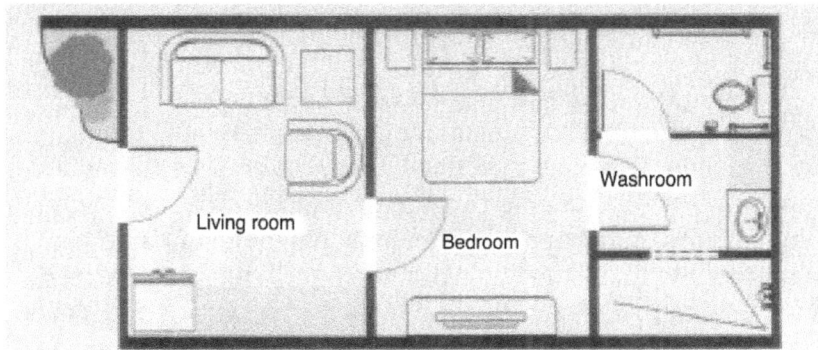

Organization Goals

- To enhance the dignity, independence, and quality of life for seniors.

- To foster interaction among seniors and between seniors and the community.

- To recruit and promote the services of volunteers from the larger community.

- To maintain a sense of usefulness and add value to their lives.

Services will include:

- A fully operational Welcome Center

- Fully furnished, double occupancy living units

- Multi-purpose lounge and entertainment area

- Therapeutic Massages

- Fully Equipped Gym

- Hair and Body Salon
- Games and Recreation Area
- Landscaped gardens and leisure areas

STAGE THREE

Skilled Senior Care Facility for seniors who need daily observation and a medical watch.

When the quality of life of a senior deteriorates to the point they are beyond the capacity of assisted living, they require more than basic services. They may not be fully ambulatory and may be unable to regulate their medications such as blood pressure medicine, insulin shots, or just unable to remember to take the right pill at the right time with food, etc. At this point these seniors need regular observation and skilled personnel to regulate their dosages and timeliness of medication. Constant observation and evaluation of their condition is required.

Directors

- Dr. Partan Balloo. Chairman
- Dr. Subesh Ramjattan, C.E.O.
- Debra Frost Ramjattan, Secretary
- Anil Ramdin
- Brian Vital
- Dr. Peter Morgan. Specialist Counsellor
- Dr. Patricia Morgan. Edu. Psychology

STAGE FOUR

A Hospice-type facility for the terminally ill will be constructed when the need is adequately demonstrated and funds are available.

~

OPEN INVITATION

We invite anyone who is interested in helping people experience the fullness of life to partner with us in the development of Olive's House.

DONATIONS MAY BE MADE TO:

Republic Bank Ltd, Tunapuna West Branch,

Bank A/C #350157394501

Contact: Subesh / Debbie Ramjattan

Phone: 1-868-376-7674 or 1-868-354-7319

Fax: 1-868-645-0612

E-mail – subesh60@gmail.com or
Oliveshouse2011@gmail.com

~

Quality of Life Bridge

ALPHA

OMEGA

CARE FOR
THE CHILDREN

CARE FOR
THE ELDERLY

BRIDGE OVER TROUBLED WATER

ADULTS

CHAPTER TWELVE

QUALITY OF LIFE BRIDGE

The Alpha and Omega

Alpha and Omega are used of Christ to denote His ever-lasting existence and means the beginning and the end. The concept of Alpha and Omega frames my spiritual work and deals with the beginning of life, the children, and the ending of life, the seniors or elderly among us. The ministry of the Anapausis Community, the childcare at the Bridge of Hope, and the personal ministry of my wife and me also deal with all ages of people. We are concerned about the quality of life for each individual regardless of age and are particularly concerned about the empowerment of couples to live a quality life. The concept of Alpha and Omega ought to be used to guide and evaluate the development of community projects and services. At the Alpha end of life's continuum are the children who must have daily care and a safe place to live and grow within a family environment; on the Omega end of the continuum are the elderly who have a right to live and enjoy their golden years in peace and safety. And in between are the adult years where the quality of life also matters.

Quality of Life

It is a firm conviction that when individuals and families show proper concern for their children and parents, the path to a life of quality is opened before them. When individuals neglect themselves, their children (or other people's children), and their parents or the elderly parents of others, they are on a slippery slope in which the end is misery and disappointment. It is also a conviction that a bridge can be constructed to assist adults over the troubled spots of life and improve both personal and professional relationships. It is a quality of life bridge.

Cradle to the Grave

My basic concern is a life of quality for everyone from the cradle to the grave. Debbie and I have invested time, energy, and resources for childcare for the disadvantaged and housing for the elderly, known as Olive's House, initiated by funds from Debbie's grandmother. Between the cradle and the grave, we are attempting to build a Quality of Life Bridge to assist various phases of business and family life. One NGO that meets at Anapausis is known as Family Life of Trinidad and Tobago. Their motto is "help for today; hope for tomorrow." They identify five stages of Family Life beyond the childcare age and develop programs and training to meet the needs of each phase. The stages of the Family Life Cycle with programs and training are:

1. Independence

2. Marriage

3. Parenting

4. The Empty Nest

5. Retirement and Senior Years.

The Quality of Life Bridge is a way to connect to various aspects of an individual's personal and professional relationships. The bridge becomes a way to link individuals to others who can assist their self-image and self-concept as a passageway to a better and improved quality of living. The Quality of Life Bridge is a way to assist individuals and couples across troubled waters and disappointment to a brighter future through improved self-confidence and improved beneficial relationships. The quality of life normally is determined by the general well-being of individuals in the normal aspects of daily life. The acrostic below identifies some of the aspects of a quality of life bridge.

QUALITY OF LIFE BRIDGE

Quality is determined by attitudes and actions

Ultimately quality increases the quantity of life

Activities to insure that daily life has value

Living a useful life produces true happiness

Intervention to adjust areas of discontent

Total life assessment to assure positive living

Yielding gracefully to aging and the future

Opportunity to grow and develop personally

Faithfulness in all personal and social relationships

Learning and sharing with others

Increasing the worth of friends

Future healthy and comfortable state

Evaluate and encourage a sense of well-being

Builds passageways to a better outlook on life

Renewing personal and social commitments

Improved intentionality of personal action

Developing problem-solving and social skills

Growing older with dignity and self-respect

Enjoying the stages of life without regret

A Daily Guide to Quality of Life

To live a life of quality, one must daily work at improving their self-image and environment by maintaining an active and planned schedule. An unanticipated event may either be disruptive or a clear and unexpected blessing. You must decide value of the event and whether or not to permit the event to alter your plans. The confused and chaotic world will occupy you with "busyness" and intrude on your plans. You must be aware of the emptiness of a busy life that leaves no time for faith, family, or friends. Always take charge of your life and surroundings and claim periods of "rest" to bring a respite and provide breathing space for a productive life. It is the "rest" in music that makes the melody. You must daily write the melody line of your life and include the "rest notes" that provide the beat and tempo for your life. This is the only way to care for your spiritual heart and insure quality in your daily living.

Caring for your Heart

Although the physical heart is vital to life, the health of the spiritual heart is essential to the quality of life. This critical aspect of living is the psychological center of emotional well-being and consists of three elements: the mind, the will, and the emotions. You must feed positive thoughts into your mind by reading good material, listening to good music, and talking with positive friends. The will is the human decision making mechanism and is cultivated by making good decisions that positively affect yourself and others. Your emotions must be controlled.

Positive Thoughts and Good Decisions

Emotional health depends on positive thoughts and good decisions plus constructive action daily that reinforces optimistic and affirmative attitudes. This works best when you remember that an attitude is a predisposition to act. A positive mental attitude provides a tendency toward feeding the best angels of your nature and breeds an optimistic and constructive frame of mind that becomes the threshold of true happiness.

Happiness is more than the Word

Real and true happiness is more than the word "happiness" alone implies. As the word is used today it relies on the little word "hap" which means "good luck or by chance." This suggests fate or luck or good fortune, and these are far from true happiness. Happenstance does not create a quality of life. Only purposeful behavior that is more than activities can bring the deep satisfaction to life that many call "happiness." But there is a more classical view of "happiness" used by the ancient Greeks that is included in the word **eudaimonia** which comes only by a life well lived based on truth and virtue. It is this classical view that identifies the quality of life required to produce a life of faith and values. These positive virtues may be enhanced or improved by both action and attitude. When real happiness comes it will be based on truth and virtue.

Attitude and Action

It seems that attitude and action are closely related. One cannot change their attitude by just changing their mind or thinking good thoughts. There must be action. For example, only a few individuals wake up each morning and really feel like jumping out of bed and facing the cruel world. In fact most of us would rather remain in bed "a little longer," but that doesn't change our mind. We still want a few more minutes. However, by acting promptly and getting out of bed, showering, and dressing for the day, one no longer wants to take a nap, but is ready for the challenges of the day. Action changed the attitude and doing something altered the predisposition to act; therefore, the path to positive daily living is an early and prompt action. Facing the world with a smile and confidence is good evidence of a life of quality.

Stop complaining - start living!

Eat Right

Physical health depends on eating right. See food as fuel for the journey, and do not use it for comfort. Eat smaller portions and include vegetables and fruits. Stop when you feel full. Overeating is a major cause of feeling bad about yourself. Eating healthy will give you more energy and assist with weight. Eating the right food at the right time in the right amount will improve blood pressure and cholesterol. It will also help prevent heart problems both physically and emotionally. Eating right is also a family event. The whole family must be involved in the proper diet and proportions to assist those who need the discipline the most.

The big question: how do we do this? Think of your plate in sections. One half is for vegetables, and the other half is for proteins and carbohydrates. If a quantity problem persists, try a smaller plate. The same amount of food on a smaller plate will look bigger and be more satisfying. If you are still hungry after one plate full, try drinking a glass of water before the meal. Eat slower, and try a salad or soup before the main meal. If you have a portion problem, permit someone else to prepare your plate and ask that they not put the serving dishes on the table. When you see more food you want more. If you need a second helping, eat more vegetables. Learn about whole grains and avoid the salt shaker. It would be of great assistance to healthy eating to learn portion size of different foods and identify the unhealthy foods that are constantly on the table or at least on the "menu." A good way is to permit someone to take your plate away as soon as you have cleared it. As long as the plate is there you will be tempted to eat more. Remember healthy eaters consider food as fuel and do not over eat. The next meal is just a few hours away.

Be Active

A healthy life requires one to be active. Just move. Walk if you can. Exercise any and every way you can. Walk outside or in the mall. Work in the yard or the garden. Ride a stationary bike. Dance if you have moves; if not, just move. Swimming or water aerobics are good. Stay safe while you exercise. You should still be able to carry on a conversation with a friend or recite a poem or song to yourself. If breathing gets hard, stop and take a 2 minute rest and begin again. Remember, walking is more relaxing when you have someone with whom to carry on a conversation. The time goes by faster, and friendships are strengthened.

Understand your Feelings

Each individual is a unique human being. There is no one else just the same; therefore, what others may say or think about you is of little consequence. You must know yourself and understand your feelings. Know when you need medication; know when food or medicine is changing your attitude or the way you deal with others. Always speak to a medical professional about this difficulty (you do not need the advice of friends). Everyone gets upset and occasionally angry or irritable, but you must know when this behavior is being produced by the way you feel. Don't forget how many people care about you. Maintain a conversational connection with as many friends as possible and still maintain your normal life. However, don't let "friends" control your life, and don't let the "telephone, cell, or the email ding" establish your schedule or the pace of the day. Get an answer machine and return calls at 10, 2, and 4 or when it is convenient. If you feel sad or down, do something, stay busy, or do something productive to bring quality to your life.

Face the Future with Confidence

Fear of the future can destroy the quality of life. Everyone has difficulties. We all grow older. Life itself is an up and down proposition. There are hills and valleys. There are good times and bad times. Just don't let life get you down. If life serves you "lemons" make lemonade for yourself and others.

Tomorrow can be better than today provided you develop a positive attitude. Expect the best and leave the rest to God. In fact, worry is taking responsibility for things that belong to others. When "something" is beyond arms reach, leave it in God's hands. Providence knows best how to handle such things. Just live day by day expecting tomorrow to be better. This will bring quality into your daily life. This is living the good life that produces quality.

What is quality? Several words assist the understanding of the concept of quality such as: **advantage, control, excellence, importance, meaning, merit, power, status,** and **usefulness**. Let us look at each of these words and see how they expand the concept of quality.

- **Advantage** – describes a plus, a benefit, an improvement.

- **Control** – includes manage, organize, direct, influence.

- **Excellence** – denotes quality, distinction, brilliance,

- **Importance** – indicates worth, value, significance, substance.

- **Merit** – involves something deserved or earned.

- **Power** – suggests energy, strength, vitality, enthusiasm.

- **Status** – shows prominence, importance, position, standing.

- **Usefulness** – designates effectiveness, convenience, helpfulness.

Qualify of Life Concerns

Listed below are a dozen areas of primary concern when considering the quality of life of adults.

- Attitude Toward Social Change

- Feelings About the Underprivileged

- Emotional Life

- Faith-based Connections

- Financial Affairs

- Health and Fitness

- Love Relationships

- Parenting Skills

- Personal Nourishment

- Social Relationships

- Spiritual Development

- Work or Professional Life

A Rationale for Dealing with Individuals

A rationale for dealing with the "Quality of Life" relates directly to the Alpha and Omega, the beginning and the end. In the work between the children and the elderly, and the Quality of Life effort is to build a bridge across the adult years until retirement. These are the most productive and problematic years of life for most people. Scripture declared, "Man that is born of woman is of few years and full of trouble." Most of the medical and religious efforts deal with these trouble. This happens when one is dealing with adults with difficulties or weakened quality of life it is usually because of poor self-image, a bad marriage, financial difficulties, or perhaps a wealthy person using money as a pacifier in an attempt to buy happiness. The truly happy people are those who serve others and put themselves in the background.

198 GOD'S WORK DONE GOD'S WAY

Evaluate the General Well-being

The term "quality of life" is used to identify the general well-being of individuals. The term is used widely in different contexts: in this case, it deals only with an intervention in the lives of individuals with general dissatisfaction with their personal or professional life. Quality of life should not be confused with the concept of standard of living, which is based primarily on income. While Quality of Life has long been both an explicit or implicit goal for my work, an adequate definition and measurement have been elusive. There are both objective and subjective indicators across a range of disciplines and scales, and recent work on the subjective well-being surveys and the psychology and philosophy of happiness have spurred renewed interest. Included in related concepts to quality is the use of faith-based principles to guide both life and living. When life is related to faith in a Higher Power as a Guide, a better quality of life is the normal outcome. General happiness is a byproduct of this quality of life.

A Quality of Life Survey

A Quality of Life survey instrument will be used as a screening tool for individuals who desire significant change in various areas of their life. Results would highlight areas that may require change to improve their quality of life. The survey instrument could gather data on the relationship between an individual's quality of life and other behaviors. This would be an assessment using indirect measurements to develop a basis for guidance and mentoring individuals and couples. Major areas for consideration would be:

- Aesthetic Satisfaction
- Benevolent Behavior
- Career/Work Satisfaction
- Communications Behavior
- Emotional Maturity

- Extended Family Relations
- Faith-based Concerns
- Financial Security
- Future Concerns
- Happiness Measure
- Health/Fitness Measure
- Inter-personal Relations
- Leisure/Vacation Behavior
- Marital Relations
- Parenting Relations
- Personal Growth
- Physical Fitness Indicators
- Security Concerns
- Self-Image Concerns
- Social Activity
- Daily Stress Level
- Sense of Well-Being

Related Concepts

Also related are concepts such as personal freedom, individual rights, and happiness that have intruded on marriage and family as well as the professional and business areas. Since so many of the indicators are subjective and cannot be directly measured, it becomes necessary to develop an instrument to surrogate these qualities and assess them indirectly. For example, "How much does a man love his wife?" This cannot be directly measured but must be indirectly assessed through a developed index.

What is obvious is that increased income or actual wealth does not directly impact the Quality of Life. Consequently, standard of living will not be taken as criteria for quality of life. Yet, several assessed areas will be considered as having some influence on the quality of life. It is my clear conviction that faith-based principles and the qualities of spiritual development can greatly influence the quality of life for adults. Adequate spiritual development can assist an individual or a couple over the troubled waters of life and bring a renewed quality and quantity to life. A survey instrument will be developed to assess the areas of weakness that impact quality of life for individuals in their marriage, interpersonal relationships, career, and professional life.

The Pursuit of Happiness

No community effort, program, or service is complete that does not take into consideration the needs of children, the elderly, and all the adult dynamics that are a part of the process from birth to death. The primary concern is for the children because they represent the future. At the other end of the journey are the elderly with their needs and wants. Also, in between the children and the elderly are the lives of many adults who live without the quality of life needed to assure that life is worth living. Some call this happiness, while others see contentment and pleasure coming from the use of faith-based principles and the addition of spiritual worship. In reality life is a journey, and the adult pursuit of happiness normally needs a little guidance to focus on the objective and proper goals in life and career. It is the pursuit of happiness. Life is not always a bed of roses. All circumstances are not pleasant, and all the people with whom we come in contact are not always filled with gladness. However, I believe there is a place, built on faith-based principles, that becomes the foundation for a life of quality and peace.

Pure Religion before God

Holy Scripture is clear that pure religion is to look after the women who are alone and the fatherless in order to keep them from being tainted with guilt. To subordinate such guilt is to bring greater condemnation upon all who neglect the needs of orphans (fatherless) and women who are struggling alone to care for their children.

Transparency in Belief and conduct

> 27. Free from all that would dim the transparency in belief and conduct before God and the Father is this, **to go see and relieve the orphans without a father's protection and the women lacking a husband in their distress,** and to keep himself untainted with guilt. (James 1:27 DNT)

AMEN

— so be it —

An expression of strong agreement and affirmation, the AMEN is an indication that the author clearly affirms the content of this book as a needed message to believers.

~

"When the Spirit and the Word burn a vision in your heart, write it down. You are ready to walk the walk and talk the talk. Faith and love have prepared you to do God's work, God's way!"

POST SCRIPT

WRITE THE VISION

A Specific and Straight Forward Plan

Without the prophetic revelation from God people will be aimless and slothful in their work for God. The plan for man is clear in God's book we call the Bible. It is specific and straight forward. A wise proverb states, "Where there is no vision, the people perish," (Proverbs 29:18). God basically said, "I have done this for you! You do this for Me, and I will do the rest." Since we are working together with God to do His work, we should write down our plan of action. It should be inscribed in our subconscious so clearly that we follow it automatically regardless of the circumstance. Controlling this written vision is the prayer:

**"GOD, SHOW ME WHERE YOUR CAUSE
NEEDS ME MOST."**

God Gave a Personal Message

During my absence from Trinidad several years ago, at a time when I was earnestly seeking guidance, I believe God gave me a personal message. An urgent call was felt to assist the less fortunate on the Eastern Seaboard of Trinidad. I realized that God was guiding me back to my old home village area of Plum Mitan. There had been a conscious avoidance of the deprived and needy in the poor villages, but a passion began to grow in my heart for the disadvantaged and underprivileged of my Homeland. I had prayed, "Lord show me where your cause needs me most," and his answer was Trinidad and Tobago. In my quiet time with God one morning these words came clearly

to me as if someone was speaking audibly to the ear of my
h**ear**t:

> "My son, My son, know that I am aware of your struggles, *but
> be not afraid; for I will give you My peace,My grace and My
> love. Be not afraid, My son,— for you will give direction to a
> lost people. Be not afraid, My son, for I will empower you."*

These words have been a guiding force to me and my wife
daily since that morning. Each time I remember them, speak
them, or write them, the episode becomes real again, and I am
encouraged to keep pushing ahead.

Come grow with me; the best is yet to be. Everything that
has happened to you before has prepared you for the next step.
It will be a step of faith, but with God all things are possible!

> *16. But this is what was prophesied by Joel; 17. When the last
> days come, I will pour out a portion of my Spirit on mankind:
> your sons and **daughters shall speak forth divine truths, and
> your young men shall see visions of prophetic significance,
> and your old men shall experience vivid images of hoped
> for things even sleeping:** 18. And on your believing servants
> will I pour out of my Spirit, and they shall speak forth under
> inspiration. (Acts 2:16-18 DNT)*

God Is No Respecter of Persons

God is no respecter of persons; each human being is
loved the same. God made "of one blood all," and Jesus was
crucified for the salvation of everyone who will hear and accept
God's call to repent and confess Christ as Savior and Lord. I
am confident as God spoke to me many years ago, divine
authority can and will speak to you. It may not be just the same
way God worked with me, because each individual is different, and God works within the framework of that individuality.
Pray, earnestly desire the true faith of the early believers, read
and study the Word of God, and you will receive a clear understanding of exactly what God wants you to do and how you

can become involved more effectively in reaching individuals and families in your community and making them into followers of Jesus Christ. When you understand, write it down. This becomes your vision, your visualization of God's call on your life. Then you can share your vision with others, particularly with those you have assisted over the obstacles and through the human maze to find Christ.

Love with the Love of God

When one is able to love others with the love of God, they are better able to follow the leading of the Spirit. This means no conditions and no decisions based on race, religion, culture, or tradition. Where the Spirit leads, believers must follow. Just because an individual may have been raised in another culture, tradition, or religion does not mean that God does not love them the same as He loves you. Deeply rooted in most of the world's religions is some form of the Golden Rule that instructs basically that one should treat others the way they wish to be treated. If you were hungry, homeless, sick, or down on your luck, how would you wish to be treated? To make this point the paragraph below shows that the principles and values that come from the Golden Rule are present in much of the ancient writings that formed the basis for culture and tradition.

The Last Word is "Grace"

"May the **grace** of our Lord Jesus Christ remain with you-Amen!" (1 Thessalonians 5:28 DNT). As one daily reads the Holy Scriptures, words and phrases seem to jump out of verse after verse; it is different ones on different days. I assume that this happens because each one of us have different needs day by day, and the Holy Spirit shines the light of truth on the path for our daily walk. Reading the last words of the old salty sailor, Simon Peter, or the final message of the Prophet to the Gentiles, Paul, or the ending of the writing of John, the last Disciple standing, the same word "grace" is there. Each of these men had difficult times in their lives, yet when Peter speaks to John Mark, or Paul writes to young Timothy, or the Old Disciple, John, writes to the persecuted believers scattered throughout the Roman Empire, the same word "grace" is part of their final farewell.

Modern English Weakens Grace

Grace is used in modern English for all kinds of attributes such as loveliness, elegance, refinement, beauty, style, poise, charm, kindness, favor, dignity, honor, and being distinguishable. Grace is used as a title of honor for royalty or a person of high rank. It is what one calls the short prayer at mealtimes. At some event when a dignitary attends, it is said that they "graced the event" by attending. These uses of "grace" weaken the meaning. In Christianity the word "grace" is the infinite love, unmerited favor, mercy, and goodwill shown to the human race by Almighty God. The concept of grace is much stronger than it is presented in modern English. In the Greek language of the New Testament the word is *"charisma"* meaning *"unmerited favor"* toward an undeserving person. The scripture declares "by grace are you saved;" this salvation was undeserved and unmerited, yet it was God's willing gift to all who believe. "Saved through faith; it was the gift of God."

Earnestly Contending with Spiritual Energy

21. And you, were once estranged and mental enemies by evil deeds, yet now you are restored as friends, 22. through the death of his earthly body, to present you consecrated and blameless in his sight: 23. **if you remain steadfast and fixed in your faith, and not removed from the hope of the gospel, which you heard that which was preached to the whole world; whereof I Paul was made a ministering servant;** *24. and now my suffering for you is a joy as I complete in my body the full story of the sufferings of Christ for the sake of his body which is the church: 25. of which I became a servant, according to the stewardship God gave me for the Gentiles to fulfill the word of God; 26. Even the sacred secret that was hid from past generations, but is now uncovered to his saints:*

27. to whom God was pleased to manifest the wonder of this sacred truth among the Gentiles; which is Christ in you, the anticipation of glory: 28. Whom we proclaim, admonishing and instructing every man in all knowledge; that we may present every man mature in Christ Jesus: 29. To this end I toil with all my physical strength, earnestly contending with spiritual energy. (Colossians 1:21-29 DNT)

Examples of Grace

Besides you and me, the Bible is filled with examples of people who have experienced the grace of God and been mercifully restored to a useful place in God's work. There is no trouble that God cannot fix. There is no earthly sorrow that heaven will not heal. There is no sin (except the sin against the Holy Spirit) that God will not forgive. Forgiveness is the essence of the nature of God. An old adage speaks to the human issue: "To err is human; to forgive is Divine!"

29. Let no unwholesome words come from your mouth, but only good words for enriching, that it may serve as a blessing to the hearers. 30. Never distress the Holy Spirit of God, whereby you have been marked for the day of redemption. 31. Let your bitter frame of mind, anger and violent outbreak or brawling, and abusive language, be put away from you with all hatred: 32. **become gracious to one another, tenderly affectionate, ready to forgive one another, even as God for Christ's sake forgave you.** *(Ephesians 4: 29-32 DNT)*

- Peter had cursed, lied, and denied Christ, yet he was welcomed back to the fellowship of disciples and then permitted to preach the main sermon on the Day of Pentecost. Most of us would have held him back because of his past behavior, but God and those who understood redemption permitted Peter to do God's work and "strengthen the brethren" after he repented and returned to the circle of discipleship.

- God placed the harlot of Jericho in the lineage of Jesus, and she appears in the list of Faith Heroes, "By faith the harlot Rahab perished not with them that believed not," *(Judges 2:1; Hebrews 11:31).*

- God used David after his moral failure as an example of a man "after God's own heart."

- God even used Solomon, the child of David's immorality, to build the Temple and become a man of wisdom. This is the grace of God at work, the unmerited favor of divine mercy.

- The redemptive mercy shown by the restoration of Peter after the crucifixion and the case of the penitent thief who was "nailed to the cross" at Calvary were examples so none would despair, but only a few examples so no one would presume or "frustrate" the grace of God.

- Saul of Tarsus, who became Paul, the Apostle to the Gentiles, was an **extreme example of grace**. He considered himself a sinner of the "first rank" because he was educated in the Jewish Law at the feet of Gamaliel, yet did not accept Jesus as the Messiah until he was struck down in blindness on the road to Damascus and led by the hand to the street called Straight to a man who prayed with him to receive his sight and be filled with the Spirit.

An Extreme Example of Grace

12. Thanks I give to the one empowering me, Christ Jesus our Lord, because he deemed me faithful putting me in his service, 13. **Who was a blasphemer, a persecutor, a man of violence, author of outrage, and yet he had mercy on me, because I was acting in the ignorance of unbelief.** *14. But the* **grace of our Lord** *was more than abundant with faith and love which is in Christ Jesus. 15. What a true saying and worthy of a favorable reception, that Christ Jesus came to* the world to save sinners; **of whom I rank first. 16. And yet I was pardoned, so that in me first Christ Jesus might give an extreme example** of his longsuffering; I was to be a precedent for all those who will ever believe in him and win eternal life. 17. Now to the King of the ages, incorruptible and invisible only God, be honor and glory unto the ages of the ages. Amen. *(1 Timothy 1:12-17 DNT)*

The Road to True Discipleship

As those you lead to Christ become growing disciples, you can walk together on the road to true discipleship and service. As you walk with Christ on life's journey and fellowship with other believers, your vision will guide you to more exciting things. When the Spirit and the Word burn a vision in your heart, write it down. You are ready to walk the walk and talk the talk. Faith and love have prepared you to do God's work, God's way!

Doing God's Work God's Way
Blessed by following the Lord's instructions

*42. So the people of Israel **followed all the Lord's instructions** to Moses. 43. And Moses **inspected all their work and blessed them because it was all as the Lord had instructed him**. (Exodus 39:42-43 TJB)*

~

As we follow the Lord's instructions, together we can do God's work God's way!

— I leave you with these words —

Come, all Christians,
Be committed to the service of the Lord.
Make your lives for Him more fitted,
Tune your hearts with one accord.
Come into His courts with gladness,
Each His sacred vows renew.
Turn away from sin and sadness,
Be transformed with life anew.
Come in praise and adoration,
All who on Christ's name believe,
Worship Him with consecration,
Grace and love will you receive.
For His grace give Him the glory,
For the Spirit and the Word,
And repeat the gospel story
Till all men His name have heard.

Text by Eva B. Lloyd

God bless you on your Spiritual journey

May God always grant you,
Light from the Word to guide you;
Faithful friends near you;
Laughter to cheer you;
A Guarding Angel, so nothing will harm you
And when you pray—Heaven to hear you!
And, may the Grace of God bless you richly?
And His Face shine upon you.
May many Christian friends support you,
And the Holy Spirit Keep you on the Straight path,
And provide you a peaceful journey, AMEN!

"So may God and our Lord Jesus Christ Himself who has showed such love to us, giving us unfailing comfort and enduring hope through His grace. Encourage your hearts and confirm you in all right behavior, action and speech,"

(2 Thessalonians 2:16, 17 DNT).

AMEN!

EPILOGUE

The author of this book is an amazing man. He was born into a practicing Hindu family in a poor part of Eastern Trinidad and left home at a young age to find his way in life. God gave him a business head, and he found his way in the world of business, in both Trinidad and the U.S.A.

One day he became a follower of Christ, which only made him a better businessman, now doing business God's way. The title of this book, *God's Work Done God's Way*, truly describes the man and his "quality of life" philosophy for all.

I personally met Subesh Ramjattan when I went to buy carpet for a pioneer church at his store in Trincity, Trinidad. It was a Divine appointment, and we have been tied together in God's work ever since. His lovely wife, Debbie, is a constant friend and companion to this man of God, and they are a spiritual son and daughter to me and my wife.

From the business world, God increased their influence to the Christian world, and the Anapausis Community and the Bridge of Hope were established. Reaching and caring for underprivileged and orphan children is part of the ministry of the Bridge of Hope. Anapausis includes training, teaching, reaching, and benefiting lives. Now, in the making, is a needed Retirement Village for the Elderly for Trinidad and Tobago, known as Olive's House.

Subesh and Debbie are making an impact for God's Kingdom and improving the quality of life for many. Their commitment is most commendable.

—Robert A. Doorn PhD,
Intl. Director of Kingsway World Missions

*For no prophecy was brought forth by the will of man at
any time: but men spoke from God being brought forth
by the Holy Spirit.*

(2 Peter 1:21 DNT)

RECORD OF EVENING & MORNING READING

You may keep a record of your reading by circling the Chapter numbers as they are completed using The Evergreen Devotional New Testament (DNT). Read the books and letters of the New Testament chronologically to get a feel of the progressive nature of God's revelation to mankind. Always keep in mind both the human writer of the passage and the inspiration of the Holy Spirit that prompted and motivated the writing of the words. There were eight (8) human writers of the New Testament; however, the Holy Spirit was the true Author. The writer is marked after the name of the Book or Letter. The code for writers is: [J] James; [JD] John, the Disciple; [JJB] Jude, Jesus' Brother; [JM] John Mark; [L] Luke; [M] Matthew; [P] Paul; [SP] Simon Peter.

Order and Record of Chronological Reading

Book	Writer	Chapters
James	[J]	1 2 3 4 5
Mark	[JM]	1 2 3 4 5 6 7 8 9 10 11 12 13 14 15 16
I Thessalonians	[P]	1 2 3 4 5
II Thessalonians	[P]	1 2 3
Galatians	[P]	1 2 3 4 5 6
I Corinthians	[P]	1 2 3 4 5 6 7 8 9 10 11 12 13 14 15 16
II Corinthians	[P]	1 2 3 4 5 6 7 8 9 10 11 12 13
Romans	[P]	1 2 3 4 5 6 7 8 9 10 11 12 13 14 15 16
Luke	[L]	1 2 3 4 5 6 7 8 9 10 11 12 13 14 15 16 17 18 19 20 21 22 23 24
Matthew	[M]	1 2 3 4 5 6 7 8 9 10 11 12 13 14 15 16 17 18 19 20 21 22 23 24 25 26 27 28
Philemon	[P]	1
Colossians	[P]	1 2 3 4
Ephesians	[P]	1 2 3 4 5 6
Philippians	[P]	1 2 3 4
Acts	[L]	1 2 3 4 5 6 7 8 9 10 11 12 13 14 15 16 17 18 19 20 21 22 23 24 25 26 27 28
I Timothy	[P]	1 2 3 4 5 6
Titus	[P]	1 2 3
II Timothy	[P]	1 2 3 4
I Peter	[SP]	1 2 3 4 5
Jude	[JJB]	1
Hebrews	[P]	1 2 3 4 5 6 7 8 9 10 11 12 13
II Peter	[SP]	1 2 3
John	[JD]	1 2 3 4 5 6 7 8 9 10 11 12 13 14 15 16 17 18 19 20 21
I John	[JD]	1 2 3 4 5
II John	[JD]	1
III John	[JD]	1
Revelation	[JD]	1 2 3 4 5 6 7 8 9 10 11 12 13 14 15 16 17 18 19 20 21 22

APPENDIX B

BOOKS BY THE AUTHOR

The Anapausis Partnership
ISBN 978-1-935434-49-8 (2011).
Common-sense lessons and faith-based principles that result in a model of Philanthropy, Mentoring and Coaching.
$16.95 USD

Living a Life LARGER Than Yourself
ISBN 978-1-935434-62-7 (2012).
The path to a life of quality.
$6.95 USD

God's Work Done God's Way
ISBN 978-1-935434-60-3 (2012).
You don't have to make headlines to make a difference.
$16.95 USD

Scheduled for 2013
Navigating the Challenges of Faith-Based Behavior
ISBN 978-1-935434-64-1

Order: **www.gea-books.com** or

From the Author: **subesh60@gmail.com** or

Amazon, Barnes&Nobel and other web sites or

Anyplace there is an Espresso Book Machine

Printed in Australia, Brazil, France, Germany, Italy, Spain, UK, and USA

APPENDIX C

ABOUT THE AUTHOR

Subesh Ramjattan is a remarkable man who is hungry for knowledge and reaches for every kernel of truth he can find from any source. His life journey began in a poor village learning common-sense lessons from h s family and the village environment. He proceeded to learn more in school and as a young man working hard to gather both the knowledge and the resources needed to start his own business. He listens to anyone who speaks and reads everything in sight. Subesh remembers almost everything good he hears, sees, or learns from any source. He is unselfish in giving resources for projects for the disadvantaged and constantly demonstrates his concern for faith-based operations and the individual believers who take an active role in faith-based groups.

Subesh is a serious student of all subjects that touch his life, business, and spiritual commitment. When he discovers the interrelationship of concepts and constructs, he desires to share them with others. This interest has resulted in a business and spiritual journey that has ncreased the quality of life for many. His first book, *The Anapausis Partnership*, co-authored with his wife, Debra, catalogued much of the business and spiritual journey that established a model of philanthropy, mentoring, and coaching to improve the quality of life for the disadvantaged of Trinidad and Tobago. The documentation of this process produced the awarding of a Doctor of Humane Letters (DHL) by OASIS University's Institute of Higher Learning.

The most meaningful aspect of the lives of Debra and Subesh Ramjattan is that they give all the credit to God for their blessings and their ability to bless others.

—The Publisher

APPENDIX D

References & Selected Reading

Barrs, Jerram. (2001) *The Heart of Evangelism*. Wheaton: Crossway Books.

Biehl, Bobb. (1997) *Master Planning: The Complete Guide for Building a Strategic Plan for Your Business, Church, or Organization*. Nashville: Broadman and Holman.

Borthwick, Paul. (2003) *Stop Witnessing and Start Loving*. NavPress.

Baxter, J. Sidlow, (1960) *Explore the Book (Volume One) Genesis to Joshua*. Grand Rapids: Zondervan.

Chittister, Joan (1990) *Wisdom Distilled From the Daily: Living the Rule of St. Benedict Today*. San Francisco: HarperCollins.

Coleman, Robert (1972) *The Master Plan of Evangelism*. Grand Rapids: Baker.

Coleman, Robert E. (2000) *The Master Plan of Evangelism*. Spire.

Craig G. Bartholomew and Michael Goheen, (2002) *Finding Our Place in the Biblical Story*. Grand Rapids: Baker.

Dallas Willard, (1998) *The Divine Conspiracy: Rediscovering Our Hidden Life in God*. San Francisco: HarperCollins.

Dallas Willard, (2002) *Renovation of the Heart: Putting on the Character of Christ*. Colorado Springs: NavPress.

Dietrich Bonhoeffer, (1985) *Spiritual Care*. Minneapolis: Fortress Press.

Dunagin, Richard L. (1999) *Beyond These Walls*. Nashville: Abingdon Press.

Eims, LeRoy (1978) *The Lost Art of Disciple Making*. Grand Rapids: Zondervan.

Eisenman, Tom. (1987) *Everyday Evangelism – Making the Most of Life's Common Moments*. Grand Rapids: IVP

Foster, Richard (1978) *The Celebration of Discipline: The Path to Spiritual Growth*. San Francisco: HarperCollins.

Green, Hollis L. (2007) *Discipleship*. Nashville: GlobalEdAdvancePress.

Green, Hollis L. (2007) *Why Churches Die*, Nashville: GlobalEd AdvancePress.

Green, Hollis L. (2010) *The EVERGREEN Devotional New Testament*, Nashville: GlobalEdAdvancePress.

Green, Michael, ed. (2002) *Church Without Walls: A Global Examination of the Cell Church*. Grand Rapids: Eerdmans.

Green, Michael. (1970) *Evangelism in the Early Church*. Grand Rapids; Eerdmans.

Harding, Kevass J. (2007) *Can These Bones Live?: Bringing New Life to a Dying Church*. Nashville: Abingdon Press.

Hunter, George G. (2000) *The Celtic Way of Evangelism: How Christianity Can Reach the West...Again*. Nashville: Abingdon Press.

Hybels, Bill. (2006) *Just Walk Across The Room: Simple Steps to Pointing People to Faith*. Grand Rapids: Zondervan.

Little, Paul. (1988) *How to Give Away Your Faith*. Grand Rapids: IVP

McQuilkin, Robertson. (1999) *The Great Omission*. Waynesboro: O. M. Literature.

Mittleberg, Mark. (2008) *Choosing Your Faith: In a World of Spiritual Options*. Tyndale House Publishers.

Moore, R. York. (2005) *Growing Your Faith by Giving it Away*. Grand Rapids: IVP

Ramjattan, Subesh and Debra. (2011) *The Anapausis Partnership*. Nashville: GlobalEdAdvancePress.

Ramjattan, Subesh (2012) *Living A Life Larger Than Yourself*. Nashville: GlobalEdAdvancePress

Ruffcorn, Kevin E. (1994) *Rural Evangelism: Catching the Vision*. Minneapolis: Augsburg.

Shakespeare, William (1623) *Julius Caesar* in the First Folio [Act 4, Scene 3]. Shakespeare never published his plays; the first printed was after his death.

Sorenson, Stephen. (2005) *Like Your Neighbor?: Doing Everyday Evangelism on Common Ground*. Grand Rapids: IVP.

Vaughan Roberts, (2002) *God's Big Picture: Tracing the Storyline of the Bible*. Grand Rapids, IVP.Wagner, C. Peter. (2006) *The Church in the Workplace: How God's People Can Transform Society*. Ventura, CA: Regal.

Wilder-Smith, A. E., (1960) *Why Does God Allow It?* Victory Press.

Wilkinson, Bruce H. (2000) *The Prayer of Jabez*. Sisters, OR: Multinomah.

GOD'S WORK DONE GOD'S WAY

YOU DON'T HAVE TO MAKE HEADLINES TO MAKE A DIFFERENCE

SUBESH RAMJATTAN

*"The grace of the Lord Jesus Christ, and the love of God,
and the fellowship of the Holy Spirit always be with you all.
Amen!"*

(2 Corinthians 13:14 DNT).

GREEN WINE
FAMILY BOOKS

www.ingramcontent.com/pod-product-compliance
Lightning Source LLC
Chambersburg PA
CBHW021052090426
42738CB00006B/301